Dudley's book gives great insight into why so many people around the world love Dolly Parton. While Dolly is one of the biggest superstars, she has never forgotten who she is and where she came from and the faith that anchors her life.

GOVERNOR OF TENNESSEE, Bill Haslam,
and First Lady Crissy Haslam

Three amazing strands of stories are woven into this fabulous book, *The Faith of Dolly Parton* by Dudley Delffs. The thread of biography speaks of a fascinating woman whom we tend to think we know, but whom I admire even more when seeing her through the lens of faith. The thread of memoir shared through the author's blending of his own life story with Dolly's is a gift of hope and connection. And the final thread, that of devotional, invites us to more. Faith-based questions at the end of each chapter take us deeper into our own stories, while the prayers remind us that it was Dolly's faith that has taken her to the heights she's attained, as she humbly acknowledges. Reading this book reminded me of my own faith journey and the gift of story told through music, words, and life. I love this book! You will too!

JANE KIRKPATRICK, award-winning
author of *All She Left Behind*

The Faith of Dolly Parton is a little book filled with big dreams! Dudley Delffs weaves together his unique spiritual journey with the wonder and wisdom of Dolly Parton's with a heartwarming result. I was uplifted by the inspirational gifts of both and delighted by the author's humor and the joy hidden in the stories of Dolly's life. Inside this book, part memoir and part biography, lies a map for readers to unfold their own prayers and dreams.

DONNIE WINOKUR, author of *Chancer:*
How One Good Boy Saved Another

You may know Dolly Parton as a legendary singer, songwriter, music producer, actor, author, philanthropist, or entrepreneur. But those external successes are born out of a deep personal faith in Jesus Christ. In *The Faith of Dolly Parton*, award-winning author Dudley Delffs guides you through ten powerful lessons based on the music, character, and heart of this entertainment legend. Delffs's insight into the sincere faith of Dolly Parton will warm your heart and inspire you to become more vulnerable as you grow stronger in your faith.

CRAIG GROESCHEL, pastor of Life.Church,
New York Times bestselling author

The Faith of Dolly Parton made me smile one minute and reconsider what I thought I knew about her the next. Dudley Delffs uses his own spiritual journey to frame the way Dolly's Christian faith has anchored her life throughout her many career accomplishments and personal milestones. The result is a warm, down-home conversation about much more than Dolly and country music, offering us a reflection on the beautiful, mysterious ways God uniquely uses each of us for his kingdom.

CHRIS HODGES, senior pastor of Church of the
Highlands, author of *The Daniel Dilemma*

The Faith of Dolly Parton

Lessons from Her Life to Lift Your Heart

DUDLEY DELFFS

ZONDERVAN

The Faith of Dolly Parton
Copyright © 2018 by Dudley Delffs

Requests for information should be addressed to:
Zondervan, *3900 Sparks Dr. SE, Grand Rapids, Michigan 49546*

ISBN 978-0-310-35292-1 (hardcover)

ISBN 978-0-310-35294-5 (audio)

ISBN 978-0-310-35293-8 (ebook)

All Scripture quotations, unless otherwise indicated, are taken from The Holy Bible, New International Version®, NIV®. Copyright © 1973, 1978, 1984, 2011 by Biblica, Inc.® Used by permission of Zondervan. All rights reserved worldwide. www.Zondervan.com. The "NIV" and "New International Version" are trademarks registered in the United States Patent and Trademark Office by Biblica, Inc.®

Scripture quotations marked ESV are from the ESV® Bible (The Holy Bible, English Standard Version®). Copyright © 2001 by Crossway, a publishing ministry of Good News Publishers. Used by permission. All rights reserved.

Scripture quotations marked KJV are from the King James Version. Public domain.

Scripture quotations marked NLT are from the Holy Bible, New Living Translation. © 1996, 2004, 2007, 2013, 2015 by Tyndale House Foundation. Used by permission of Tyndale House Publishers, Inc., Carol Stream, Illinois 60188. All rights reserved.

Scripture quotations marked TPT are from The Passion Translation®. Copyright © 2017 by BroadStreet Publishing® Group, LLC. Used by permission. All rights reserved. thePassionTranslation.com

Any internet addresses (websites, blogs, etc.) and telephone numbers in this book are offered as a resource. They are not intended in any way to be or imply an endorsement by Zondervan, nor does Zondervan vouch for the content of these sites and numbers for the life of this book.

All rights reserved. No part of this publication may be reproduced, stored in a retrieval system, or transmitted in any form or by any means—electronic, mechanical, photocopy, recording, or any other—except for brief quotations in printed reviews, without the prior permission of the publisher.

Interior design: Kait Lamphere
Cover photo: Emma Stoner / Alamy
Butterfly image: © vectorgirl/Shutterstock

First printing April 2018 / Printed in the United States of America

Contents

Introduction: The Butterfly Effect 7

Chapter 1: Dream Your Way Forward. 13
Chapter 2: You Need Wings to Fly 37
Chapter 3: Know When to Stretch Your Wings 61
Chapter 4: Love like a Butterfly While Busy as a Bee. .83
Chapter 5: Practice More Than You Preach 107
Chapter 6: Baby Steps toward a Leap of Faith 133
Chapter 7: Let Your Roots Keep You Grounded. . . .153
Chapter 8: Shine through the Shadows. 173
Chapter 9: Laugh First to Make Love Last 193
Chapter 10: Read into the Future 213

Acknowledgments. 229
Notes 233

INTRODUCTION

The Butterfly Effect

> *I always ask God to work through me and let me be a light of some kind and help in this world, so I always pray for that, and I always want to do good.*
> DOLLY PARTON

I love Dolly Parton.

I grew up with her, really. Dolly graduated from Sevier County High School the year I was born, which technically makes her old enough to be my mother. But to me she seemed more like an extended relative—a favorite aunt or beloved cousin. While I'd have loved for her to be my godmother, like she was for Miley Cyrus's character in *Hannah Montana*, Dolly hovered at the edges of my life, part muse urging me to dream more and part guardian angel pulling me back to my roots.

As a boy growing up in small-town Tennessee, I spent many evenings sprawled on the pea-green carpet of our family room watching Dolly on *The Porter Wagoner Show*, my daddy's favorite. Later, as a young man I prepared to propose to my wife beneath the watchful gaze of Dolly's bronze statue in front of the courthouse in Sevierville, Tennessee. And as a young father, we took our three small children on vacation to Dollywood.

I've never met Dolly in person and have only seen her perform live a couple of times. But like the University of Tennessee, the Smoky Mountains, biscuits and gravy, the works of Flannery O'Connor, and the lonesome sound of the night train echoing from beyond the pasture on the farm where I grew up, Dolly Parton is woven into the fabric of my life. And it's not just her music that has shaped who I am—it's her Christian faith.

When I talk about the spiritual role models in my life who continue to inspire me, most people laugh or raise their eyebrows when I include Dolly on that list. But why not? In a world filled with so much turmoil, division, strife, and conflict, Miss Dolly models a kind of Christian faith that manages to be authentic, positive, hopeful, and contagious. In a world where public figures fall from pedestals daily, if not hourly, Dolly Parton is the exception. She keeps the faith, holds her ground, and keeps on being who she has always been ever since rising into stardom over fifty years ago. Whether celebrating a new album or unveiling an addition to her eponymous theme park, Dolly has never been shy about crediting God and her relationship with him as the source of her success. Even when others prefer to focus on her iconic curves, the

The Butterfly Effect

mysteries of her love life, or her latest groundbreaking endeavor, Dolly still manages to give God credit for it all.

More important than what she says, though, is how Dolly lives out her faith in tangible, openhearted, mountain-moving ways. She's a philanthropist and a humanitarian—big words for a little lady who says she only wants to share her songs with as many people as possible. There's a simple childlike joy about her generosity and desire to help other people, whether teaching children to read or enabling residents of her beloved Smoky Mountains to recover from devastating wildfires.

Dolly doesn't preach or presume to tell us how we ought to think and behave. She doesn't discuss denominations, politics, or other people's mistakes. If anything, she goes out of her way to take the high road, to give people the benefit of the doubt, to hope for the best in her fellow human beings. Dolly frequently quotes the Bible but has refused to be baited by matters of interpretation or theology. She keeps her faith simple, mostly private, and action-oriented.

She's a "Backwoods Barbie" as fervent as Billy Graham, but Dolly would never set herself up as a spiritual role model. Yet you will struggle to find a better example of what it means to be hugely successful and still humble, gifted yet grounded, both faithful and fabulous, as genuine as they come despite the glamor, a cultural icon yet still a simple gal from the holler down near Locust Ridge. Positive and profound, upbeat and down-home, sequins sparkling on an old soul, Miss Dolly can teach us a few things about accepting ourselves, loving others, chasing our dreams, trusting God, and celebrating the life he has given each of us.

Her lessons of faith are often small and subtle, which reflects what Jesus said about giving: "When you demonstrate generosity, do it with pure motives and without drawing attention to yourself" (Matthew 6:3, TPT). The way Dolly Parton lives out her faith reminds me of the butterfly effect. Borrowed from science and mainstreamed into pop culture, the term *butterfly effect* usually refers to the way small, seemingly trivial events—such as a butterfly flapping its wings in one location—can have enormous consequences, contributing to a tornado, for instance, in another part of the world.

I can't think of a better metaphor for Dolly's faith and its cumulative impact on millions of lives. Her faith demonstrates the effect small habits and patient dedication to one's dreams can produce. Captivated by butterflies since chasing them as a girl, Dolly was inspired to write and record her hit song "Love Is Like a Butterfly," gradually adopting the little winged beauties as her brand symbol and personal totem. When asked why she loves butterflies so much, Dolly said, "They remind me of myself . . . they just go about their business, gentle, but determined."

No doubt about it, Dolly's gentle, determined way of living out her faith has pollinated so many people's lives, including my own, with joy, inspiration, and hope. She has become known for her compassion, generosity, inclusivity, and philanthropy as much as for her voice, musical artistry, and famous figure. The positive impact of her music, personality, storytelling, songwriting, and generosity is undeniable. She makes me proud to be from Tennessee, to love country music, and to be a Christian.

Whether you're just discovering Dolly or are a lifetime admirer of the Queen of Country, I hope you will be encouraged, inspired, amused, and energized by the life lessons that follow, all drawn from Dolly's life. I don't know her personally and she hasn't paid me to say nice things about her. If anything, she would probably joke about much of what I have to say and then change the subject to talk about her new album or the latest books donated to kids participating in her Imagination Library. That's just who she is. She would be the last person to make a fuss about her faith.

But that's the very reason we love her. Hers is the kind of faith that inspires you to be all that God made you to be. The kind of faith that can help you hang on when times are hard and to set your sights higher after your latest accomplishment.

She models the kind of faith that takes big leaps, gets back up after a fall, and trusts God for the next giant step. The kind that causes you to pray, to really talk to God openly and honestly from your heart again. To keep quiet around others if you can't say something nice.

To pause and marvel at purple wildflowers swaying on a sun-kissed hillside.

The kind of faith that hums a little song through the darkest night and still finds something to laugh about when there are plenty of reasons to cry. The kind of faith that celebrates blessings and joyfully shares them with others.

The kind of faith that lasts a lifetime.

The kind of faith this book is all about.

The faith of Dolly Parton.

CHAPTER 1

Dream Your Way Forward

In the midst of the direst poverty and despair, the human spirit, especially that of children, will find some hope to cling to, some promise of a better day.

DOLLY PARTON

I'll never forget the first time I saw Dolly Parton.

I was probably about six at the time, sprawled on the carpet of our family room—the den as we called it—arranging green army men among plastic farm animals and Matchbox cars while my parents watched shows on the large oak-veneered RCA console angled in the corner. Our viewing skewed toward my father's favorites or shows considered appropriate for our family, which basically meant me as the only kid in the house and my parents' only child together.

The same shows always seemed to be on: staples like *The Andy Griffith Show* and *Gunsmoke*, along with *Bonanza, Mannix,* and *Hawaii Five-O*. Two country music shows, however, stood out: *The Porter Wagoner Show* and *Hee Haw*. While my father loved country music, these programs didn't interest me much. Some of the music was okay, even good sometimes, but the country cornball humor annoyed me.

I couldn't put my finger on it at the time, but the corny jokes and predictable routines puzzled me. They were goofy and silly, playing up the stereotypes that even as a kid I found over-the-top and limiting, if not insulting. My father tended to laugh, especially if he was on his third or fourth drink, and my mother would grin or chuckle, usually following his lead.

Despite my usual disinterest in what my dad was watching, one person on *The Porter Wagoner Show* always drew my attention. I know it's easy to assume that I was fascinated by her extraordinary figure and frothy blonde hair sculpted like cotton candy—and maybe I was—but there was something special about Dolly Parton. I couldn't have put it into words then, but it was more than just the fact that she was young and pretty and had big breasts. It was even more than her beautiful voice that reminded me of birdsong, sometimes bright and chipper like a robin and other times as lonesome and sad as a whip-poor-will.

Yes, Dolly had—for lack of a better word—*presence*,

that mysterious star quality exuding from certain people who seem more alive, more aware, more positive, basically, just *more*. Many of these larger-than-life people are entertainers, performers, and celebrities, but many wait tables, manage retail stores, or repair computers. I suspect Dolly would still be Dolly even if she were a bank teller, a soccer mom (now there's an image!), or an attorney.

Whether performing a duet with Porter or pretending to be a dumb blonde in a hillbilly skit, Dolly seemed both smart and sincere. She didn't mind poking fun at country stereotypes because she was in on the joke. She was self-aware enough to deliver her punch lines with that tinkling-bell laugh of hers and then emotionally intense enough to beg "Jolene" not to take her man and mean it. The fact that she wrote many of her own songs only reinforced my impression that she was not like every other performer or country music singer.

Simply put, Dolly was special.

Humble Beginnings

Dolly's origins have become the Smoky Mountain mythology her brand is built on. She has always joked about it ("Sure we had runnin' water—when we'd run and get it!"), but the reality must have been severe. Working their small farmstead from a two-room cabin in the shadow of the Great Smoky Mountains, her parents,

Lee and Avie Lee Parton, focused on keeping food on the table and a roof over the heads of their growing family. They were so poor that the local doctor who delivered Dolly, Dr. Robert Thomas, received a pound of cornmeal as payment.

One of Dolly's earliest biographers, Alanna Nash, then a journalist for *Country Music Magazine*, visited the old Parton cabin and wrote: "No matter how many pictures you have seen or how much you have fantasized about it, you are not prepared. It is the most extreme rural poverty imaginable—direr even than Dolly has painted it—and as you stand there gazing at the ancient washing machine on the porch and the inoperative still off to the side of the house in front of the rusted automobile parts, and the scraggly chickens, you feel guilty for having wondered if Dolly has exaggerated her humble origins."[1]

Dolly's father raised a bit of tobacco as a cash crop, tended the family's vegetable garden, and worked construction and odd jobs in nearby Sevierville and Knoxville to keep his family going. Mama Parton stayed home with their young children, keeping them all clothed and fed while often expecting their next one. Early on she disguised their poverty through her imagination, teaching Dolly and her siblings how to make "stone soup," turning a meager broth with potatoes and a few vegetables into a magical meal.

By virtually all accounts, little Dolly was a happy, carefree child, usually running barefoot in the swept, dirt-packed yard, chasing after chickens or listening to her mama tell Bible stories from their tiny porch. She had older siblings to play with and younger ones to chase after. Nonetheless, as the fourth of twelve children, Dolly also realized early on that her parents simply didn't have the time or energy to devote to each child's specific preferences, talents, and personality. "[Daddy] and Mama had so many kids that none of us got special attention."[2] But what they did have, she's always quick to add, is plenty of love. Dolly and her siblings knew what being in a loving family was all about.

Photograph of Dolly (upper right in the back) and family at Christmas in 1960

And Dolly quickly found a way to stand out. Music became her natural means of self-expression, a shared language that commanded the attention of her family, friends, and neighbors. Whether at home doing chores, worshipping at church, or performing at school, Dolly's sunny smile and crystal clear voice could not be ignored.

Even before she was born, Dolly was surrounded by music. Her mother frequently sang hymns and old mountain folk songs to her children while cooking, doing chores, and sewing by the fire. Her maternal grandfather, Reverend Jake Owens, was a Pentecostal preacher, so Dolly was exposed to more hymns and church music in the tiny mountain church where he preached. She was singing in church by age six and playing guitar by age seven.

And it wasn't just to get others' attention. Writing songs and singing them was as natural to Dolly as breathing in the fresh mountain air. She's made up little melodies for as long as she can remember, with "Little Tiny Tasseltop," a song about a beloved corncob doll her mama made for her, being the first song she ever wrote. Young Dolly noticed the natural rhythms around her while growing up—the two notes of a bobwhite, the sound of her mother snapping beans, the tap-tap-tap of a spoon on a cup—and found herself humming and riffing throughout the day.

Dolly knew she loved music and never thought about whether it was practical. With the joyful assurance of a child doing something she loves, Dolly never questioned her attraction for words set to music. She just seemed to know that songs and singing were part of who she was, part of who God made her to be.

Dolly enlisted her siblings, especially her sisters, to join in her performances too. She even jokes that her sisters were "musically abused" by Dolly's attempts to make them her backup singers. But she would perform even when she couldn't find an audience, well, at least a human audience. In her autobiography, *Dolly: My Life and Other Unfinished Business*, Dolly recalls how she'd stand on their front porch, grab a broom handle or tobacco stake to use as her microphone, and sing her heart out to the hens, roosters, ducks, and pigs roaming in the yard. She wrote, "They didn't applaud much, but with the aid of a little corn, they could be counted on to hang around for a while."[3]

Her Little Old Chapel

With no formal training or professional instruments, Dolly still managed to practice her songwriting and singing skills daily. When she was around twelve, she began to regularly visit an old abandoned chapel in the mountain community not far from her home. There she discovered a kind of sacred space to think about herself, her life, her dreams, and her faith.

She also discovered an old busted piano. Keeping the loose ivory tops of keys as treasures, Dolly also took some of the piano strings and fastened them to an old mandolin she'd found in her family's barn. She describes the result as sounding more like a dulcimer than anything else, but she used this improvised instrument to write many of her early songs.

Curiously enough, this deserted, run-down little church became a kind of Pandora's box for a girl on the cusp of becoming a woman, for in it her three passions, or three "mysteries" as she has described them, collided and converged: God, music, and sex. In her autobiography, Dolly describes how this little chapel became the place where she reflected on her growing attraction to boys, aided by some graphic graffiti left by some of her peers, as well as the place where she met God at a deep, personal level.

Dolly had plenty of exposure to matters of Christian faith by this point. After all, her grandfather was a preacher and her mother was a "devoutly religious woman." Dolly witnessed the way their faith worked for them. But the notion of God as an angry old man throwing lightning bolts down at sinners that she'd heard about in Sunday school and in her grandpa's sermons didn't appeal to her. Dolly describes herself as "the ultimate nightmare for a fundamentalist Christian out to save souls. I was a kid with her own opinions." She explains, "Like everything else in my life, I found God in my own unique way."[4]

Coupling her contrary nature with the unique mix of curiosity and embarrassment most of us experience going into adolescence, Dolly struggled to understand why

Christians seemed to condemn something as powerful and natural as physical attraction and sexual feelings. She grew up on a farm in a rural community and had seen plenty of animals coupling and bearing their young. It was just part of the cycle of life.

She was also keenly aware of her own developing body, and the increased attention she was receiving from boys—especially at church. Apparently, it was no accident that lots of local boys showed up on the Sunday Dolly was baptized, drawn more by the image of her rising from the water in the white sundress her mother had made than by the desire to share hallelujahs for her salvation. The church ladies noticed, of course, and made their judgment known regarding the kinds of boys these were, but they also judged Dolly for being so young, nubile, and beautiful.

Could it be true that loving God and loving boys didn't mix? And yet both kinds of love, the spiritual as well as the physical, stirred up such deep feelings. So for Dolly, it seems that her budding interest in sexual feelings got intricately tangled up with her feelings and impressions of God. That is, until she began seeking time alone with God in that deserted little chapel.

She describes the way she would sing songs to God, talk with him, and share her heart while sitting alone inside the cool shadows of the decrepit sanctuary: "One day as I prayed in earnest, I broke through some sort of spirit wall and found God. Away from the stares of boys and the mothers and the preachers, I had met him not as a chastising, bombastic bully but as a friend I could talk to on a one-to-one basis. He is our father, after all, and that's the kind of heavenly father that made sense to me."[5]

Many Christians would label Dolly's encounter with God as her moment of conversion to a personal relationship with her Creator. But this meeting was about more than her salvation; it was about her purpose. During this encounter with God, Dolly also had another epiphany. She realized that her dreams of making music and becoming a star were not silly and childish but "grand real schemes ordained and cocreated by my newfound heavenly father." She concludes, "The joy of the truth I found there is with me to this day. I had found God. I had found Dolly Parton. And I loved them both."[6]

Dolly never focused on what she lacked in her early life. She consistently chose to be thankful for what she had and chose to trust God for more. Living by faith, she has seen God bless her in ways she never imagined.

My "Testimony"

Where I grew up, we called personal stories of meeting God and getting saved "testimonies." Like Dolly, I struggled to make sense of what I heard about God in church. There seemed to be a big dividing line in the Bible. The Old Testament God seemed scary, inconsistent, arbitrary, controlling, and willing to harbor a grudge for quite a few generations. In the New Testament, God seemed accepting, forgiving, compassionate, and loving—to the point of sending his only Son, Jesus, to live as a man and to die on a cross so we could enjoy an eternal relationship with him.

I'm sure the church in which I grew up was a fine church in many ways, but like many communities of faith, it struggled with welcoming and loving people who were different. It was made up of strictly Baptist, white, blue-collar, heterosexual, teetotaling, Bible-reading families—and divorces were frowned upon. While my family ticked some of those boxes, we missed a few. Both my parents had been married and divorced before marrying and having me. While they were working class, my father didn't fit in with other fathers who were salesmen, mechanics, managers, or farmers. And unlike those folks, he was a drinker.

While working construction on a government project, my dad suffered a crane falling on his leg, which led to disability for the rest of his life. But you can't keep a good hillbilly down, so my dad found other ways to fill his time and attempted to make money in addition to his pension. He was a redneck entrepreneur: buying, fixing, and selling used cars; buying, repairing, and selling antiques, and gambling—on football teams, cockfights, pool games, dog races, and poker games. The fuel for such unique endeavors was usually beer but occasionally something stronger.

My mother and her parents were strong people of faith, born and raised Southern Baptists. Though my father was similarly raised, as an adult he had rejected organized religion. He knew the gossip and secrets of most people in our small town and scoffed at their pretense of being devout Christians on Sunday mornings when he knew what—and who—they had been doing the rest of the week.

But my parents threw a wild card into the deck from which the cards of my faith would be dealt. They made the decision to send their only son to a small Catholic parochial school in a town nearby. What possessed them, other than the Holy Spirit, to send me there and pay monthly tuition of thirty-five dollars a month, we still don't know.

What they told me was that they wanted me to have opportunities they never had. They wanted me to do better than scraping and scrounging from paycheck to paycheck. Education was vitally important. They wanted me to go to college someday. As a result, I attended the School of the Good Shepherd and received one of the best early preparatory educations available. I attended Catholic school through eighth grade before attending the local public high school.

As one of only a handful of Protestants among several hundred Catholic students, I attended mass most every day along with my classmates. I sat in on catechism and confirmation classes. I learned to say the rosary (despite my grandmother's warning not to pray to the Virgin Mary) and began collecting favorite saints like other kids collected baseball cards.

There was a sharp contrast between the faith system at school and the one at church. The mystery, the beauty, the history of the Catholic Church and its Liturgy appealed to me. I liked the way the priest used real bread and wine instead of crackers and grape juice for communion. I liked the smell of incense and the intricacy of the nativity scene during Advent and the stations of the cross during Lent.

Although I joined the Baptist church and was baptized into it as a twelve-year-old, I rebelled in my heart until my junior year of college, when I encountered God while sitting alone in a small, dark chapel at the Pope John XXIII Catholic Student Center on the campus of the University of Tennessee in Knoxville. The private conversation I had with God that day remains a turning point, one in which I found my salvation as well as my sense of purpose in the world.

Like Dolly, I rejected much of what I grew up experiencing in my local church and school and found my own personal path to God, with help from so many godly people over the years. I take to heart Paul's words to believers in the church at Philippi to "work out your own salvation with fear and trembling" (Philippians 2:12, KJV). I suspect Dolly would too.

We all have various events, experiences, and individuals that have shaped what we believe about God and how—or if—we live out our faith. Whatever your faith background, regardless of the positive and negative associations you may have with organized religion or institutions of faith, Dolly's story reminds us to embrace the unique relationship each of us is called to have with God. To approach him not as a bully or curmudgeonly tyrant but as a loving, generous, compassionate heavenly Father. To seek him in the quiet, still places of our lives.

Dreaming Is Free

Discovering her own unique relationship with God wasn't the only way Dolly overcame the expectations and limitations into which she was born. The poverty she experienced seems only to have made her more determined to succeed. Being poor wasn't a barrier any more than being female, young, or blonde. They simply were part of the world as she knew it, the same world that inspired her to chase butterflies, hum little tunes, and make up words to them.

Dolly knew she had something to give. She knew she didn't want to be contained by the mountains, living the life she witnessed growing up there. At the same time, she knew the Smoky Mountains and being "country folk" were parts of her, foundations shaping who she would become. Dolly writes, "Being born poor is something I am neither proud nor ashamed of. I have found that poverty is something you don't really realize while you're in it.

At least not if you're a kid with a head full of dreams and a house full of loving family."[7]

For me, and I suspect many of her fans, part of the magic of Dolly's story is that she grew up about as poor as one can be. She's never tried to sugarcoat it, and while she often jokes about it, she also tries to avoid romanticizing it. She shares stories of how, during particularly lean times, her mama would send the kids out to look for stones to make "stone soup." So caught up in the fairy tale of finding the perfect magic stone to season their supper, Dolly and her siblings shifted focus from their empty bellies to the thin soup made with little more than potatoes and onions. She has plenty of other stories, and they have become an integral part of her iconic status.

While I was fortunate to grow up in a lower middle-class family, I know my father grew up in similar conditions to those Dolly experienced. My dad was one of five and grew up in a small farmhouse in rural Bedford County, Tennessee. He grew up with no electricity or indoor plumbing. His father was a carpenter by trade and did odd jobs when he was sober enough to hold a hammer without his hands shaking. His mother sewed and did leather work for the burgeoning Walking Horse industry there in Shelbyville.

Like J. D. Vance describes in his recent bestselling memoir *Hillbilly Elegy*, my upbringing could have led me to a very different, dark, dead end. While my childhood wasn't nearly as chaotic and traumatic as the one he describes, I endured the abridged version, never sure what I'd find when I came home from school or what my father's mood and sobriety level would be.

Would he be sober, and therefore tense and angry, or would he be on his second six-pack, which meant mellow and talkative? Would he be using his .22 to shoot wasps off the ceiling in our dining room? Or would he order me to our back barn to feed and water more than two hundred roosters he was grooming for the next big cockfight that weekend?

With an unstable home life due to my father's drinking and gambling, I might have turned to alcohol, weed, meth, or a host of other illicit substances to numb my pain. Instead I channeled my energies into my education—that escape hatch my parents opened by sending me to Catholic school. Instead of pouring myself into music as Dolly had done, early on I discovered I had a gift for writing—stories, poems, school papers, jokes and riddles, really anything that could be put into words.

I was a good student, smart enough to skip grades, and basked in the academic affirmation. I was going to college come hell or high water, and I was going to make something of my life. I would write books someday, the same kinds of books that inspired, entertained, and informed me of a bigger, brighter world. I would have a different kind of life than the one my parents and most of my peers accepted.

A Patchwork Past

One true story about Dolly Parton's childhood has reached nearly mythic status—and tells us a lot about her resilience at a young age. Dolly's desire to be noticed and feel special didn't go entirely unnoticed. With the love and intuitive wisdom only a mother could possess, Dolly's mama knew the perfect way to delight her little girl and help her stand out. Mrs. Parton brought a beloved Bible story—one that's also about someone wanting to feel special—to life when she used a box of fabric scraps to make a special coat for Dolly.

The implied parallels to the biblical character of Joseph, who was his father Jacob's favorite, could not be missed. For one thing, crafting such a garment took considerable time—a precious commodity for the mother of such a large family.

But the result was worth it. Little Dolly loved the handmade gift. She describes how she couldn't wait to wear it to school and have everyone notice her beautiful coat, a one-of-a-kind symbol of Dolly's bright personality.

But when she did, her classmates didn't appreciate her new crazy-quilt jacket. Instead they teased and bullied her about it. With the vicious cruelty that kids seem to reserve for those who dare to be different, they told her it looked homemade, nothing more than a bunch of old rags stitched together.

Dolly's heart was crushed, but she loved her beautiful

coat and refused to take it off the entire day. She did not let the jeers, taunts, and bullying of her classmates deter her. For her, the coat represented the love of her mother, a recognition of her uniqueness, and a sense of her divine destiny. She wouldn't give her peers the satisfaction of turning her against it.

Dolly tells of how she walked home from school that day with her head held high, showing God her coat and knowing that he delighted in its vivid colors and the love-stitched care with which it had been made. She knew he thought she was special because he had made her that way. Despite the cruel teasing of others, she refused to be tainted by shame.

Coat of Many Colors

The story doesn't end there, of course. Dolly transformed the pain of that bittersweet memory by writing and recording the hit song, "Coat of Many Colors." "[It's] still my favorite song that I ever wrote or sang," Dolly shared in her autobiography.[8] No wonder then, that this incident became the basis for the recent television movies about Dolly's early life, "Dolly Parton's Coat of Many Colors" and "Dolly Parton's Christmas of Many Colors: Circle of Love," both on NBC.

While it's easy to romanticize the past when looking back from a more prosperous present, Dolly's song does more than honor a special childhood memory. Deceptively simple and straightforward, the poignant lyrics of her song place us as listeners in her hole-worn shoes. The song transcends the incident it recounts to reveal a deeper revelation. For the heart of the song is that Dolly felt rich in her new coat even as those around her mocked her for what their limited thinking deemed poor. Through the song, she tells us she tried to make her classmates see that one is only poor if they choose to be—coincidentally pointing out the same timeless truth to you and me.

This truth is at the center of Dolly's success. She knew even as a little girl that "the LORD does not look at the things people look at. People look at the outward appearance, but the LORD looks at the heart" (1 Samuel 16:7). None of us wants to be judged, labeled, or dismissed based on how we look or the ways others perceive us. We want to be known for what's on the inside, for the unique, special creation God has made each of us.

Through her words and in her music, Dolly consistently reminds us all to embrace our dreams in a big old bear hug of perseverance and possibility. Despite the poverty into which she was born and the hurtful attitudes of many around her, Dolly would not be deterred in pursuing her dreams. As one biographer observed, "With an active imagination, Dolly, the child, was able to transcend her desolate surroundings and circumstances, and before long, that imagination and unyielding faith provided a way to spare her the bleak future that seemed so certain to be hers as a woman of the mountains."[9] Simply put, Dolly had faith that God was doing something bigger in her life than anyone could see.

Dolly's story inspires me. I'm reminded that no matter our external circumstances or what haters might say, I never want limitations to define me. I want to pursue my dreams, confident of God's unique plan for my life. Dolly's example inspires us all to use our gifts to reach beyond where we start and to look ahead at where we're going. No matter what we're up against, we can dream our way forward.

Divine Dose of Dolly

*"For I know the plans I have for you," declares the L*ORD*, "plans to prosper you and not to harm you, plans to give you hope and a future."*
JEREMIAH 29:11

At the end of each chapter, you will find a few questions and exercises to help you apply Dolly's inspiring lessons to your own life and journey of faith. You don't have to write your answers down, but you might be surprised how helpful it can be if you do. Dolly has frequently said how much she loves making lists and how important it is for her to write down her dreams.

You'll also find a relevant theme song from Dolly's discography that you're encouraged to listen to in order to enhance your appreciation and understanding of Dolly and how she expresses her life and faith through her music. A couple questions for reflection are also provided for your consideration after listening to the suggested song.

Finally, you'll find a short prayer to adapt and use as a model for your own time of "talkin' with God." These prayers are mine, inspired by what I've learned from Dolly, both throughout my life, as well as while writing this book. There's nothing magic about my words here, but I hope they'll kindle a spark to ignite your desire to talk to God. None of this is intended to be homework but just a way of enriching your personal experience and strengthening your faith.

- What childhood dreams does the story of Dolly's coat of many colors stir in you? What incident, conversation, or gift from your childhood stands out in your memory as one that has sustained you through hard times?
- What unfulfilled dreams do you still harbor from childhood? What's one small goal you can set and pursue today to rekindle your passion from when you were young?

Listen to Dolly sing "In the Good Old Days (When Times Were Bad)" before answering the following questions.

- What feelings stirred within you as you listened to this song? Why?
- Do you believe we tend to romanticize our past and the hardships we've endured? Based on the words

Dream Your Way Forward

in this song, which Dolly indeed wrote, how do you think she regards her early struggles in light of her present success?

Dear God,

You're in charge. You've made me and brought me through good times and bad to where I am now. Help me see past the limitations in my life and focus on your many blessings. Thank you for the talents and resources you've poured into my life. Give me wisdom about how to use them to be the best version of myself—the person you created me to be—so that I may bless others.

Amen.

CHAPTER 2

You Need Wings to Fly

You're not going to see your dreams come true if you don't put wings, legs, arms, hands and feet on 'em.

DOLLY PARTON

To hear Dolly tell it, there was never a time in her life when she wasn't performing music. Already making up her own little songs and singing them, Dolly naturally sang in church, especially considering her granddaddy, Jake Owens, was the pastor at the little country church. She's often said she began singing hymns up front when she was only six or seven, and as she began to learn how to play guitar, she soon accompanied herself during the services.

By age ten, Dolly had made a huge leap from singing in church to performing on the radio. Thanks to her mother's brother, a talented singer-songwriter named Bill Owens, whom she called Uncle Billy, young Dolly encountered a golden opportunity to begin her professional singing career by becoming a regular on *The Cas Walker Farm and Home Hour,* a local radio and TV variety show there in East Tennessee.

If you study the life of Orton Caswell "Cas" Walker, it's easy to understand why he agreed to hire Dolly Parton for his show. Born into a working-class family in Sevier County, Tennessee, Mr. Walker had begun chasing his dream at a young age, quitting school at just fourteen. He then spent almost a decade working a variety of jobs, including coal mining in Kentucky, to save money to open his first Cas Walker's Cash Store in Knoxville. Eventually, he would open over two dozen such stores in East Tennessee, Eastern Kentucky, and Southwest Virginia. Always looking for novel ways to promote his brand, Mr. Walker started his own local radio, and later television, variety show.[1]

I grew up in Middle Tennessee about a hundred miles southeast of Nashville, so we didn't have Cas Walker's stores. But my wife grew up in Knoxville and vividly remembers the colorful, cantankerous, controversial Cas as the epitome of the Southern, racist, conservative, Baptist, self-made man. His stores, along with his advertising and his radio and TV programs, reflected down-home, straight-talking, working-class values accentuated with sensational, attention-grabbing gimmicks.

A master salesman and consummate promoter, Cas Walker may have been as impressed by young Dolly's work ethic and attitude as he was with her talent. As Dolly

You Need Wings to Fly

recounts in her autobiography, her uncle Bill, who had taught her how to play the guitar and shared her passion for music and stardom, took her backstage to meet Mr. Walker, where she promptly declared, "Mr. Walker, I want to work for you!"[2] According to Dolly, Walker was impressed with her choice of words, claiming that many people asked him for a job, but virtually none offered to work *for* him.

He hired ten-year-old Dolly on the spot.

Dolly describes her first public performance, there in Knoxville in the small WIVK studio auditorium, as terrifying, exhilarating, and ultimately addictive. It was as if she knew she was lighting a fuse that would result in a life-transforming explosion of the talent, dreams, and determination within her tiny frame. Starting out tentatively, Dolly owned the opportunity and poured her heart into it, claiming to sing with the same gusto she exuded in her barnyard performances back home. She admits that for all she knew, this might be her one and only chance to sing on the radio. She held nothing back, and the live audience there loved her for it.

She was an instant hit. The audience went wild and demanded an encore, which Dolly had not thought to prepare. Guided by Uncle Bill and her own instincts, Dolly sang the same song again to even more thunderous applause. She claims that incident began her love affair with the public, one she knew she would have for the rest of her life. Keep in mind, this was long before the breakout success of incredibly young talents like Tanya Tucker, LeAnn Rimes, and Taylor Swift.

This story amazes me. While we may not have the same kind of dramatic opportunities to advance our dreams like Dolly experienced that day, we can all be reminded to give all we've got when we finally get our shot. We may be nervous, self-conscious, and afraid of messing up and blowing the opportunity. But all the more reason to make the most of every moment, every encounter, every blessing that opens up before us. As Jesus said, "All things are possible for one who believes" (Mark 9:23, ESV).

Fool for Words

While I didn't have a big break at such a young age like Dolly, I probably wrote as often as she sang. I've been a fool for words and stories for as long as I can remember. I read everything I could get my hands on—blowing past Dick and Jane stories once I discovered a pig named Wilbur and a spider named Charlotte, among others. I read chapter books at school, true adventure tales from the library, *Highlights* and *Grit* in the doctor's office, and whatever I could find at home. Naturally, I tried my hand at imitating most everything I read.

Such practice surely made a difference. In his bestselling book *Outliers*, Malcolm Gladwell asserts that a person must invest at least ten thousand hours in practicing their talent or art in order to excel and maximize their potential. While some experts dispute his claim, Dolly Parton certainly provides ample evidence about what it takes to be the best.

Of course, Dolly began singing and writing songs before she started school, so accumulating those hours may have been easy. For the rest of us, though, such an investment of time and energy sounds daunting and prohibitive. And if we haven't yet invested that much time into fulfilling our dream—if we've even identified what our dream is—then we may feel like it's too late.

The trick, I suppose, which Gladwell and others have explained, is not to make the hours the point but simply steady practice in the pursuit of one's passion. If you love to draw and paint, then you'll naturally pick up a pen or brush and start doodling and sketching. If you love to cook, then no one will have to tell you to experiment with flavors to create your own recipes. And if you love music as much as Dolly, then you don't have to be forced to practice your piano lessons or come up with lyrics for your own songs.

While Dolly wasn't my inspiration at the time—more likely it was Franklin W. Dixon and *The Hardy Boys*—I too discovered my lifelong passion for writing stories early in life. Comic books, mostly Batman and Spider-Man, were also part of my steady story diet. And I'm sure the Bible stories I frequently heard at both church and school fueled my imagination as well. I can remember in Sunday school marveling at Jonah's deep dive with the whale, Noah's willingness to build an ocean liner–sized boat before it even started raining, David's courage and giant talent with a slingshot, and Joseph's coat of many colors—the catalyst, along with his big dreams, for the life of constant cliff-hangers into which his brothers sold him.

With so many heroic tales floating around inside me, it was only natural that I started writing my own. In fact, I wrote my first book to fulfill a fifth-grade class assignment. Crossing over from English class, where we wrote our story, to art class, where we illustrated and bound our book, my first (and only) Andy Archer mystery took the boy sleuth out West (from his small town in Tennessee) to his uncle's dude ranch, where he solved *The Mystery of the Copper Canyon*. While the clunky writing and yellow-daisy wallpaper book jacket still make me cringe, I can't deny how that first story foreshadowed my love for Colorado and the West, where I lived for almost twenty years, and my love of mystery novels, including a couple I wrote that were published.

Throughout my adult life, I've been most fortunate to earn a living by relying on words. But it hasn't always been easy. As Dolly frequently says, "If you want the rainbow, you gotta put up with the rain."[3]

I remember running into quite a few rain clouds in college. My roommate at the University of Tennessee majored in business, and he used to tease me about being an English major. "What can you do with a degree in English? What does a bunch of poetry and old novels have to do with real life?" he would ask. I had plenty of answers for him but harbored my own fears about being another wannabe writer or starving artist.

They're probably the same fears my future father-in-law, Jim Scruggs, had when I asked for permission to marry his daughter. At the time, I was finishing a master's degree in English with an emphasis on writing poetry. I had a university job as a teaching assistant that covered my tuition and paid a small stipend in exchange for helping teach freshman writing courses. "I'm not sure how poets make a living," Mister Jim said diplomatically. "Do you set up shop and hang out a shingle or what?"

I focused on the "or what" and continued to teach at the university level while completing a PhD in the field of creative writing. I also began getting a few poems published and started freelancing as an editor and contract writer. When I was twenty-five, a publisher offered me a contract for my first novel. An editor had read a handful of sample pages from my portfolio and loved it. Overnight, I had a contract for my first book even though the manuscript was only half finished!

With the publication of *Forgiving August*, one of my childhood dreams came true. I had always imagined I would spend years and years writing my first novel and then endure more years of countless rejection slips before a publisher took a chance and published my book, which naturally would turn out to be a bestseller. But my dream didn't happen that way. I got an opportunity that allowed me to take a giant stride on my journey but with a different outcome than imagined.

Despite selling about ten thousand copies and being optioned for a movie by a production company in Hollywood, my novel didn't launch my career as the next Ernest Hemingway or Harper Lee. In fact, not much changed other than wanting my dream—to write for a living—to come true more than ever and glimpsing just how hard it is to make it happen. But having one book under my belt allowed me to get a literary agent and contracts for more books. Getting my first novel published wasn't the doorway into fame and fortune as much as a stepping-stone in my apprenticeship as a working writer.

Just like Dolly's first big break was only the first step in a lifelong journey.

The Greased Pole of Success

While Dolly's debut on Cas Walker's show was a hit and kept her performing weekly, she describes another incident with the legendary entrepreneur that I find even more revealing—and entertaining. As one of his promotional stunts, Walker had taken an old telephone pole and sanded it smooth before staking it in front of one of his stores and coating it with grease. A cash prize of $250 sat at the top for anyone who could successfully climb the greased pole and retrieve it. This daunting task invited gawkers and lots of attention, just as Cas had planned.

But no one was able to retrieve the prize money. Until Dolly set her mind to it.

In typical Dolly fashion, this self-proclaimed tomboy and future star knew climbing to the top of the pole required more than physical strength and agility—it required cunning. Little Dolly drenched herself with water before rolling around in dirt and sand to create adequate friction for her climb. The crowd that gathered to watch her initially laughed at her tactics but then cheered as she reached the top, grabbed the cash, and shimmied down.

Back on the ground, however, someone recognized Dolly as a performer on Walker's show and started complaining that her success was rigged. As word spread the crowd became angry at what appeared to be a setup, yet another of Cas Walker's gimmicks to attract attention, having a little blonde girl accomplish what many adults had tried to do and failed.

But Walker wasn't having any of their back talk! According to Dolly, Cas seemed just as angry as the crowd, offended at their accusations that he would rig the stunt. He challenged them to prove how such a feat as climbing a greased pole could even be rigged. And in complete candor, Walker admitted he hadn't expected anyone to successfully scale the pole and claim the cash prize. He praised Dolly's ingenuity and said the money was hers to keep.

This story tickles me because it shows the shrewd intelligence of Dolly Parton in action at a young age.

Many people saw the pole and assumed it was impossible to climb. Others saw it and thought they could use sheer strength and willpower to ascend and claim the prize. But only Dolly thought through what was actually required to get the job done. She knew from others' failed attempts that strength, agility, and determination weren't enough. Something was needed to counteract all that grease coating the pole. Her method was brilliant in its simplicity. The dirt and sand clung to her clothes because they were wet. The thin layer of mud coating her body provided enough resistance to leverage her efforts successfully.

She used the resources at her disposal to create a way to reach her goal.

Dolly did what others said couldn't be done.

And she's been doing it ever since!

The Climb Continues

Dolly's climb to stardom may have begun in Knoxville with Cas Walker, but her next step required even greater courage, confidence, and calculation—and a trip to Lake Charles, Louisiana. Another of Dolly's uncles, John Henry Owens, lived there and, like his brother Bill, Uncle John loved to write songs, perform and record them. When he was stationed at a military base in Lake Charles, Henry discovered a small recording studio nearby, Goldband Records, and befriended the owner, Ed Shuler. It seemed to Dolly like the perfect place to record her first single.

You Need Wings to Fly

But first Dolly had to get from East Tennessee to Southern Louisiana. Her parents were reluctant at best, so Dolly manipulated her grandma Rena to accompany her on the Greyhound bus. Writing about that trip, Dolly makes it sound like quite the adventure and ultimately a life-changing passage. They had to change buses and, of course, missed their connection. But nothing deterred Dolly from yet another opportunity to see her dreams get off the ground. I suspect she would have carried her grandma if she'd had to in order to record her first single.

For the first time, Dolly left Tennessee and traveled through Alabama and Mississippi to Louisiana. There in Lake Charles, she recorded "Puppy Love" (a song she'd cowritten with her uncle Bill), discovered how much she loved bananas (eating too many and getting sick on them), and experienced her first true crush after meeting a dark-eyed Cajun boy, the son of Ed Shuler, the studio owner.

Her single got local radio play, mostly based on her regular appearances on Cas Walker's show, but it likely fueled her next giant—and I mean *Transformers*-sized—leap: performing onstage at the Grand Ole Opry in Nashville. I'm still stunned when I think about a girl of thirteen setting such an audacious, out-of-reach goal—let alone doing it. But then, Dolly clearly knew that the only way to make her dreams come true was to do the hard work of supporting them from the ground up.

She was determined to fly.

The Grand Ole Opry

Exactly how a young teenage Dolly landed on the stage of the Grand Ole Opry remains a bit of a mystery. She and Uncle Billy had been traveling to Nashville on weekends, meeting industry insiders and trying to give their demos to record producers. They also looked for venues that would let them perform, but most clubs wouldn't let minors in the door because they served alcohol. Although Dolly had already started maturing into her famous figure, she was still a few years away from eighteen, the legal drinking age in Tennessee at the time.

Uncle Billy already knew many country performers, both established names as well as other up-and-comers, which is likely how he finagled the favors that got him and Dolly backstage at the Grand Ole Opry one Friday night. That night's schedule had already been determined, of course, with some performers going on more than once. Which is apparently how Dolly got to take center stage.

Told by stage manager Ott Devine she was too young to perform, Dolly later said, "But I didn't give up that easy. And my uncle and me kept talkin' to everybody backstage, worryin' 'em to death, I'm sure. But finally, Jimmy C. Newman gave me his spot. He had done one spot and he had a second coming up. I don't know why he did it—out of the goodness of his heart, I suppose, but it's somethin' I'll always remember and thank him for."[4]

You Need Wings to Fly

None other than the Man in Black, Johnny Cash, introduced her, saying, "We've got a little girl here from up in East Tennessee. Her daddy's listening to the radio at home and she's gonna be in real trouble if she doesn't sing tonight, so let's bring her out here."[5]

Dolly sang a George Jones hit, "You Gotta Be My Baby," and the response was much like the first time she sang on Cas Walker's show. The crowd went wild and she performed three encores.

I don't know how to convey just how huge this was. The Grand Ole Opry is one of those revered institutions that somehow deserves its iconic status, sustained by decades of talented musicians, singers, songwriters, and performers, each generation's legacy strengthening the next. Started in 1925 by Nashville radio station WSM, the program began as an hour-long "barn dance" that included mostly bluegrass, folk, and country.

By the time Dolly performed in the late 1950s, the Opry had established itself as the premier showcase for country music. It had expanded to four hours and broadcast live from the Ryman Auditorium each weekend. Shows featured chart-topping country music stars as well as new breakout talent—like young Dolly—on their way up. Both regional and national products sponsored the Opry, including Martha White Flour, Prince Albert Tobacco, Pet Milk, Coca-Cola, and Purina. Now known as "Country Music's Most Famous Stage," the Opry prides itself on crossing genres, hosting performers singing and playing bluegrass, folk, gospel, rockabilly, and pop—all within the vibrant, dynamic canon of authentic American music.

I grew up listening to the Grand Ole Opry on the radio in my daddy's old GMC pickup on Saturday nights when he and I went hunting or fishing together. It's one of my best memories of feeling connected to him when I was growing up. Daddy loved the great female singers like Patsy Cline, Loretta Lynn, and Tammy Wynette, as well as George Jones, Jim Reeves, and Roger Miller, whose hit "King of the Road" we'd sing together.

His favorite was Hank Williams singing "I'm So Lonesome I Could Cry," which I couldn't understand at the time, but later, as an adult, it made perfect sense. All that suffering, anguish, and pain laid bare in the stark beauty of simple words and images. For me, that may be the essence—and the brilliance—of the art form known as country music: transforming personal pain into shared beauty. Soulful lyrics telling a story set to rhythm and melody. Giving voice to the unspoken heartache of millions of listeners.

Even when the music wasn't to my liking on the Opry, I still appreciated the diversity of performers and styles. Most of all, there was just something electric about hearing a live performance only eighty miles up the road from where we lived. It made me feel connected to a time and a place, to people before me and beyond me. Those songs I heard as a boy with my daddy made the world seem bigger than Franklin County, Tennessee, and somehow also more bearable.

I wonder if Dolly had similar feelings that night she performed. If she realized how quickly her dreams were taking flight. If she had any idea how high she would go. That night Dolly unveiled her voice, her talent, her presence, her sheer force of will in being there in a way that no one could forget. She had laid the foundation for the dream that would continue taking shape before her very eyes.[6]

Elbow Grease

With a regular, weekly radio gig, a recorded single, and a stunning debut at the Grand Ole Opry, it's no surprise that Dolly's next step was to move to Nashville. She had promised to finish high school first, which she did and became the first in her family to do so. Despite her early successes, though, her classmates laughed when Dolly announced her plans to go to Nashville and become a big star after graduation. At the time it hurt her feelings, but later she reflected that her peers simply didn't have the capacity to take her big dreams seriously. If you can't imagine yourself leaving home, taking risks, working hard, and persevering when times get hard—all in pursuit of your heart's desire—then it's difficult to understand how anyone else could. But Dolly got on a bus with her guitar and three grocery bags full of her belongings the very next day after receiving her diploma from Sevier County High School.

For all of her incredible breaks while so young, Dolly still faced innumerable barriers once she landed in Music City. Knocking on doors, shoving demo records in producers' hands, hitting the pavement day after day, and looking for the next gig had to be exhausting as well as humbling. Despite her early successes, she was just like so many other young, hungry, talented artists trying to make it big in Nashville.

With the ongoing assistance of her devoted uncle Bill, Dolly persevered and did all the grunt work that most people experience when attempting to launch a career in the arts and entertainment. They kept plugging away, day after day, week after week. They continued writing songs, staking out opportunities to meet influential movers and shakers in the industry, and seizing every chance to take another step closer to stardom. They would wait for hours in a record executive's office based on his polite invitation the day before to "drop by" sometime.

During this time, Dolly worked part-time jobs when she could, babysitting and waiting tables mostly. But money was tight, and she later joked about living on ketchup and relish, even going into a grocery store and pretending to shop just so she could down a pint of milk or sneak some chips. Weeks turned into months, and many others would have given up and taken the next bus home. But not Dolly—she was there for the duration, determined to make it one way or another.

Finally, her hard work began to pay off, and Dolly landed spots on early morning Nashville radio shows hosted by Ralph Emery and Eddie Hill, respectively. Around the same time, something even more significant happened: she caught the eye of Fred Foster, the owner of Monument Records and Combine Publishing, who signed her to a deal. While Foster initially envisioned Dolly as a female Elvis, he came around to see her true potential after another artist, Bill Phillips, had a big hit with "Put It Off Until Tomorrow," a song written by Dolly and Uncle Bill that went on to win BMI song of the year in 1966. Dolly harmonized vocals on that song, which went uncredited but created quite a buzz among those in the industry.

Based on this buzz and Dolly's own preference, Foster agreed to let her return to singing and recording country songs. It was the right move. Back in her comfort zone, Dolly had her first top ten country hit with "Dumb Blonde," a prophetic song if there ever was one. It's a breakup song, but the feisty lyrics could easily be Dolly's motto: "Just because I'm blonde/Don't think I'm dumb." In fact, she later joked that it never bothered her when anyone called her a dumb blonde because she knew she wasn't dumb—or blonde!

The Engine of Faith

Getting your dreams off the ground requires more than hard work—it takes faith. You have to believe not only in your own talent and ability but also in God's ability to do more through your life than you can do by yourself. About this season of her life, Dolly later said, "I had this something that kept pushing me forward even when I was so scared I wished I could die. It was something I had to do, not because somebody else had told me I had to, but because I had told myself I did."[7]

Dolly's dreams may have been fueled by her hard work, but the engine for pushing herself and persevering had to be her faith. She knew she wasn't the prettiest or most talented and certainly not the richest or best connected. But she knew she had been given something special by God—something she felt compelled to share with others, the gift of her music. Maybe it's a calling or just living out the purpose you were created for, but regardless of the label, it comes back to trusting God.

The Bible is filled with stories of men and women who weren't the best or smartest, the richest or most educated, but more times than not, they are the ones God chooses to bless and shine through. They are simply willing, sometimes reluctantly, to follow God's path while being good stewards of all the Lord has given them. From Abraham to the apostle Paul, from Rahab to Ruth, the leaders we find fulfilling their divine destiny in the Bible all have one thing in common. It's not their external appearance or internal intelligence that fuels their success. It's not their family connections or large inheritance. It's their faith.

What is faith? "Faith is confidence in what we hope for and assurance about what we do not see" (Hebrews 11:1).

You Need Wings to Fly

With this definition established, this passage from the Bible then lists a Who's Who of the Old Testament, identifying well-known believers who trusted God for amazing, usually miraculous results. The factual evidence may not have supported their goal. The resources available to them might not have been enough. The logic of their situation might have dictated the exact opposite of what they knew they had to do—because they lived by faith and not by sight.

Believing in God and trusting him for your own good may not seem easy at first. But maybe this kind of trust in him is like a muscle we develop over time—and it does get easier to rely on him if we're exercising it consistently. Maybe that's the benefit of spiritual disciplines as they're usually called, those habits and practices designed to deepen our faith and draw us closer to God. They help you discover your purpose in life and the joy that comes from living out that purpose for the benefit of those around you.

Dolly Parton understands this as well as any preacher I've ever met. In her book *Dream More*, Dolly reveals that she once asked her mother why she thought God had blessed her with such extraordinary success and not others she knew who were smarter or more talented. Mama Parton said, "God has his purpose for everybody. We all have our journey to walk."[8] She went on to tell her famous daughter that she suspected God had blessed Dolly with so much because he knew Dolly would be willing to share.

Joy in the Journey

I like that answer. Sure, we can all point to lots of successful people who don't seem half as generous or caring as Dolly. But I seriously doubt any of them are truly happy and enjoying what they have. So many successful people seem to lose sight of their blessings and become fixated on the next big thing—their next big promotion, accomplishment, conquest, purchase, or privilege. You know, the "I'll be happy when" phenomenon. Only, the when never arrives, and enough never seems to be enough.

I've tried to keep this in mind as I've slowly advanced and experienced what most people would consider a successful writing career. It's not the fame and fortune of John Grisham or the prestige and pedigree of Joyce Carol Oates, but it's allowed me to do what I love doing—writing, telling stories, helping others tell their stories—and has provided a decent income for me and my family. I'm incredibly blessed to be my own boss, work with amazing authors, and make a good living. And my journey isn't over yet!

Neither is yours. A few years ago, I reached a milestone birthday and struggled with the knowledge that, most likely, more than half my life was over. While some of my dreams have come true, I was forced to acknowledge that the odds were against me fulfilling others, such as writing my own superhero comic book, penning an Academy Award–winning screenplay, or hitting the *New York Times* bestseller list for a book with my own name on it and not someone else's.

I moped for a couple of weeks, but then I saw Dolly being interviewed about a new TV movie she'd produced based on her life, *Dolly Parton's Coat of Many Colors*. Not only was she excited about this movie because of its deeply personal story line, but because she genuinely wanted to encourage people that nothing is impossible. If a sharecropper's daughter from Locust Ridge could become arguably the most glamorous and successful woman on the planet, then anything could happen. Dolly also announced she was about to launch a new album, *Pure & Simple*, and begin her largest world tour in twenty-five years, performing in over sixty cities.

I had to laugh at myself and quit moping.

At a time in life when so many people are content to enjoy retirement or, like me, are lamenting unfulfilled dreams, Dolly was taking risks and going strong. She hadn't quit dreaming or stopped working hard to see new dreams come to life. Her example inspired me to drag out a screenplay I'd started years before and had never finished. Maybe it was too late for me to take home an Oscar someday, but I would never know if I didn't try, would I? Dolly's example cuts through my excuses like a hot knife through butter!

Her work ethic reminds me of a marathon runner, pacing herself mile after mile, knowing when to go a little faster or a little slower, conquering hills and enjoying the view along the way. Sure she can sprint, but her ultimate goal requires a steadier, more consistent pace to reach the destination that remains miles away. Like the writer of Acts, she can say, "My only aim is to finish the race and complete the task the Lord Jesus has given me—the task of testifying to the good news of God's grace" (Acts 20:24).

Dolly illustrates running the race of faith to which we're all called, stepping out and trusting God to lead the way. She reminds us that if you work hard and patiently persevere—and if you keep the faith and trust where God is leading you—then your dreams eventually take flight. But you'll never fly if you don't try!

Divine Dose of Dolly

*May the favor of the Lord our God rest on us;
establish the work of our hands for us—
yes, establish the work of our hands.*
PSALM 90:17

🦋 How much effort do you put into pursuing your dreams each day? What often prevents you from working harder and devoting more time to what you care about most? How can you draw on your faith in God to overcome these obstacles?

🦋 What were your favorite pursuits, hobbies, and interests during childhood? Music, sports, fashion, animals—something else? What did you enjoy learning about the most when you were growing up? What have you done to cultivate your interest in these areas lately? What's one thing you can do today?

Listen to Dolly sing "Better Get to Livin'" before answering the following questions. You might want to look up the lyrics as well, just to make sure you hear all that Dolly has to say in this song.

The Faith of Dolly Parton

- How do Dolly's lyrics in "Better Get to Livin'" speak to you considering where you are in your life right now? How does that make you feel? Why?
- Do you agree with Dolly in this song that it's always easier to complain about our lives than to work toward our own happiness? What would it look like for you to "get to livin'" and pour more of yourself into the pursuit of what matters most to you?

Dear God,

Sometimes I feel foolish when I consider my childhood dreams in the midst of all the cares and responsibilities in my life now. But you made me for a special purpose and you've given me dreams that may seem dead but are only sleeping. Awake those dreams in me, Lord, and show me the steps I need to take to realize those dreams. Give me your power to keep going when times are hard and give me your peace when troubles come. I know my dreams can't come true unless I rely on you.

Amen.

CHAPTER 3

Know When to Stretch Your Wings

You may not want to be a star, but you do want to star in your own dreams.
DOLLY PARTON

One night Dolly appeared on our TV screen in a flowy red dress and looking as solemn as Sister Ann Thomas, our school principal, during morning mass. Dolly sat on a little white bench and sang a song we'd never heard before. It was called "I Will Always Love You," and she sounded sadder than the First Baptist Church choir singing "How Great Thou Art" at my granddaddy's funeral that year. At one point the screen split, showing off the new advancements of technology, and Dolly appeared to be singing to herself. She didn't cry or get teary, although she looked and sounded like she could, with her trembly vibrato. Despite the sadness of the song, I sensed maybe she really wasn't that sad at all.

Porter Wagoner and Dolly Parton, 1973

Porter, decked out in an outfit that looked like a rhinestone factory exploded onto his blue leisure suit, joined Dolly immediately after her performance. He said, "I think that's one of your prettiest songs."

"Thank you," she said.

"And you sang it like you meant it," he added.

"I did mean it—I do."

Turned out Dolly was leaving *The Porter Wagoner Show*. My father couldn't believe it. But my mother had no trouble at all.

"He *made* her a star—she'd be nothing if not for Porter. I can't believe she thinks she can go off on her own and make it," Daddy said as if he himself had been personally betrayed by Dolly's departure from the show. This would've been in 1974 when I was ten years old.

"She's smart," my mom said without looking up from the magazine she was reading. "Dolly Parton will make it just fine without him."

"Naw, she'll come crawling back—you wait and see."

I assumed Dolly and Porter were married and so all this business about Dolly leaving must have to do with divorce, something I knew my own parents had been through before. It was my secret fear whenever they started fussing and fighting. Later, of course, I learned that Dolly and Porter shared a business partnership, professional collaboration, and personal friendship, though there was plenty of speculation about what went on behind closed doors. I didn't say anything at the time, but whatever their breakup was about, I agreed with my mother. With all due respect to the great Mr. Wagoner, I had no doubt that the pretty blonde lady with the big hair, big voice, and big bosom would be just fine.

Leaving the Comfort Zone

I'm not sure what compelled Dolly to make such a bold career move other than her own creative instincts. Many people would have been more than happy to keep the good times rolling, the hit songs coming, and the bucks in the bank. By her own admission, Dolly owes Porter a huge debt of gratitude for furthering her career and increasing her visibility before millions of fans. But as she's also quick to point out, Porter didn't discover her—she credits her uncle Bill Owens with that honor, thanks to his years of loyal support—or make her a star. Dolly's light was already shining bright and flying high when he invited her to replace his former female sidekick and costar, "Pretty Miss Norma Jean" Beasler, not to mention all the hard work Dolly had invested in expanding and diversifying her success.

Dolly provides great insight in comparing her time with Porter to being a student in an accelerated school. While she was already a singer, she credits her Missouri mentor with making her a true performer: helping her to read an audience, connect with the crowd, bond with fans, and handle all the things that come up during a live performance. Being on a hugely popular show with a veteran country star must have been like graduate school for Dolly—and she passed with flying colors.

But the goal of going to any school and getting an education is to graduate. Commencement, it's called, that milestone of recognizing how far you've come as you look ahead at all you want to do. Like any relationship between strong-willed, talented, smart people, Dolly and Porter's partnership likely had its share of conflict, criticism, and competition. They've both acknowledged experiencing the ups and downs that come from any shared commitment to a common goal. But I suspect as their success grew, and as Dolly looked ahead and saw her thirtieth birthday just around the corner (she was twenty-eight when she left Porter's show), she realized she was at a crossroads.

I suspect Dolly simply reached a tipping point where it was clear that Porter's goals and dreams were not her own. He envisioned enjoying and sustaining what they had built together and continuing to sing, perform, and record the music they loved. In a male-dominated field, he likely imagined remaining in control of the decisions, the vision, and the power in their partnership. Perhaps he assumed Dolly was willing to "stand by her man," too comfortable in his shadow to risk standing alone in the spotlight.

Dolly, however, has never seemed afraid of taking a risk. She's enough of a contrarian to question Porter's control and to chafe at his constraints. She's also strong, stubborn, and smart enough to know when she had learned all she could learn from her former teacher. Dolly wanted more than to maintain the successful career she'd built—she was just getting started. All she had achieved was merely a foundation for what was yet to come: starring in her own show, acting in movies, headlining national and international tours, and writing more songs, and telling more stories in as many ways as possible.

Public speculation and industry gossip about the Dolly-Porter breakup spread like country western wildfire and continues to this day. They were linked together the same as Loretta and Conway, Tammy and George, even Sonny and Cher. Many of their fans were crushed by Dolly's decision to step away from her longtime duet partner.

Porter didn't take the news well either. Maybe he thought she was bluffing and he could win the poker game by calling her bluff. But when she followed through with leaving and launched her solo career, Porter Wagoner was furious. He sued Dolly after she left, demanding three million dollars and a percentage of all her future earnings as a performer. She was devastated, not by his financial demands but by the way he was claiming credit for her success. It was the last nail in the coffin of their relationship.

Looking at her options, Dolly took her attorneys' advice to settle out of court and pay Porter a million dollars just to make the lawsuit go away and move on with her life. While we might assume such a payout wasn't difficult to make for a big star like Dolly, in later years she revealed that this settlement basically wiped her out. Like many successful performers, she didn't have liquid assets to draw from and instead had to scrape together all she and her husband Carl had at the time. "I made up my mind that if he [Porter] could live with it, I could live without it."[1] Dolly wanted a clean break from Mr. Wagoner and knew that this was ultimately a small price to pay for her creative and professional freedom.

It was a huge step of faith, but one she felt compelled to take.

It was time to stretch her wings and see how high she could fly.

Opportunities to Stretch

I have no delusion that my humble career as a writer can compare to the stellar success blazed by Dolly's supernova. But I have faced my share of turning points at various crossroads in my life. One of the most dramatic was leaving the academic world and my love of teaching in order to pursue a career in publishing. Looking back I find it makes sense, but at the time I worried that I was selling out.

I was in my midthirties and had accepted that I would be a college professor, teaching various writing and literature courses, and writing novels on the side. Although I had a couple of master's degrees, the small Christian university in Colorado where I was teaching required a terminal degree, in my case a PhD in English, in order to advance to a more secure position as a full professor. I was just finishing that PhD at the University of Denver, where I was blessed with an incredible community of supportive, inspiring faculty and students, when I received the job offer.

My wife and I had just had our third child, and I was our sole breadwinner. The new position, fiction editor for a Christian division of Random House, would literally double my teaching salary overnight. Plus, I figured I could always go back to teaching and academic life if I didn't fit in the corporate world. Most of all, as a fiction editor I would still be directly involved with words and bringing stories to life. And for someone who loves books as much as I do, it was ultimately like offering someone with a sweet tooth a job in a candy store—irresistible.

But I still faced a challenging time of transition. For the first time in my adult life, I would no longer be on a college campus, either as a student, grad student, or faculty member. I had an entire new world to learn about, one I knew and loved from the outside, but now I was behind the curtain helping the wizard. My boss at the time liked to joke that publishing was like making sausage—lots of people love the result, but few can stomach the process of how books are made. The corporate perspective, as opposed to the personal or academic, was about making money, not necessarily making the best book. I encountered many people, including my boss and executives in New York, who didn't care much about what was in a book or even what it looked like as long as it sold well and was profitable for the company.

I'm an idealist though. I believe the best way to make sure a book sells is to focus on its quality. Considering this very book you're now reading as an example, you might laugh. But I'm not talking about trying to make every book or piece of writing into literature (said with a British accent). I simply mean making each book the best at what it's intended to be, whether it's an Amish romance novel, a self-help guide for improving your finances, a memoir about your marriage, or a Bible reference book.

This motivating standard of excellence was soon

Know When to Stretch Your Wings

tempered by realistic practicalities such as deadlines, launch dates, and budgets. But my love of books and ability to navigate the business and administrative side along with the editorial and marketing side led to rapid advancement. After successfully growing our company's fiction program and dramatically increasing its revenue, within three years I was named vice president and editor in chief. While I was excited to have even more influence on which books we would publish, I also knew I had a lot to learn. Leading a team and managing people required much more time and energy.

Or, as Dolly might say, flying high feels great until you hit the ceiling!

Crossing Over

After her break with Porter, Dolly wasted no time getting off the ground again. She made one of the greatest decisions of her career by hiring high-powered Hollywood manager Sandy Gallin. By Dolly's account, the two of them were about as different as pork rinds and Perrier, but they hit it off instantly. Already representing stars such as Cher and Joan Rivers and entrenched in the L.A. scene, Gallin immediately shared Dolly's vision for a career beyond country music. He recognized her intelligence, work ethic, and creativity, as well as that ineffable quality that makes some stars burn brighter than others.

Dolly was already starting on a new album, and her

new manager found the perfect song to help her stretch her wings. The title of both the album and the chart-topping first single released, "Here You Come Again" catapulted Dolly beyond country and into popular, mainstream markets. The result was her first album to sell over a million copies, a Grammy Award, and several successful singles (including "Two Doors Down"), and the Country Music Association's highest honor, Entertainer of the Year.

As with any major transition, though, Dolly experienced plenty of growing pains. Many country fans worried that she was leaving them behind for popular approval and mainstream airplay. In addition to signing with a Hollywood agency and releasing a pop crossover album, Dolly had also made some changes with her band. She disbanded the Traveling Family Band, which indeed featured mostly Parton relatives, and put together a more musically eclectic group called Gypsy Fever to keep up with her new style. I suspect this change ruffled some feathers, including with some people close to her. Her new direction caught the attention of mainstream media, though, landing her a full-length interview in *Rolling Stone* (although she lost the cover to a quartet of characters from that summer's big blockbuster, a space western called *Star Wars*).

Despite such changes, Dolly repeatedly reassured fans and critics alike that she was still the artist she had always been. "I'm not leaving country music," she said, "I'm just takin' it with me to new places."[2] For Dolly, it was simply about having creative freedom to make all kinds of music and not getting locked into one genre and style. It was about exploring her own maximum capacity for creativity. In the *Rolling Stone* interview, she told writer Chet Flippo, "This is a new freedom for me. Just total self-expression and daring to be brave, just to really see music the way that I totally feel it."[3]

Keeping the Faith

In that same interview, Dolly's faith was front and center. In addition to noting how easily she often quoted from the Bible, Flippo asked Dolly about her extraordinary positivity. "I was born with that gift and that great faith," she replied, "and it wasn't until about two years ago that I discovered that there were books written about positive thinking. But, you see, I had practiced that all my life, *that's* what got me out of the mountains. Even as a little child, I daydreamed so strongly that I just saw these things happen and sure enough, they would . . ."[4]

It's not just her powerful imagination, though, that fueled Dolly's ascent. She explained, "We can be whatever we want to be, the Bible says that, that *all* things are possible to those that *believe*. It don't say *some* things are possible, it says *all* things are possible and it says that if you have faith even as a grain of mustard seed then you shall move mountains and that nothing shall be impossible unto you."[5]

At this crucial juncture of her life, Dolly almost takes her faith and positive thinking for granted. How could she make such big leaps of faith if she didn't have faith in God and faith in herself? They are such a core part of who she is, habits ingrained from her upbringing in a loving family and her grandpa Jake's church, as well as a reflection of her sunny personality. It's almost as if she can't understand why everyone doesn't grasp the truth that's right there in the Bible, in Matthew 19:26 and 17:20 to be precise. "That [capacity for faith to do the impossible] is within *everybody*. People just neglect what they got to work with."[6]

I agree, although I can see how others might interpret Dolly's belief in the power of faith differently. They might question the implication that our faith can get us anything we want, reducing God to a magic genie who grants our wishes whenever we rub the lamp of faith. But I don't think this is what she's getting at. Dolly assumes that the mountains most people would want to move would be for the benefit of everyone, not just for their own gain. Knowing the Bible as well as she does, Dolly understands, "When someone has been given much, much will be required in return; and when someone has been entrusted with much, even more will be required" (Luke 12:48, NLT).

Was Dolly focused on being successful, famous, and rich? Without a doubt. Did she have more in mind than just acquiring wealth and a lot of material possessions?

Know When to Stretch Your Wings

Absolutely. She had dreams to provide jobs for thousands of people in the impoverished area where she grew up, to offer educational opportunities for children around the world, to help anyone in need, and to inspire everyone with her music. As a naturally giving person, Dolly knew that the more she received, the more she could give. And to this day, her generous heart continues to bless millions of lives with the contagious kindness she's practiced her entire life.

So often I have neglected to remember that the loving power of God is able to do the impossible in my life. In the midst of unexpected hardships—my battle with depression or my wife's fight with cancer, I find it easier to worry, doubt, and fear than to keep the faith and trust God. Even when new opportunities present themselves, such as when I went to work in publishing, I sometimes struggle to remember Who opened the doors that I walked through to get to that point.

I love the way Dolly, over forty years ago, cited her faith as the key to her success. Dolly reminds me and all of us that God's power to do the impossible is not a one-shot event but a limitless source. Launching into all her new ventures after leaving Porter Wagoner, Dolly still declared, "I ain't *near* where I'm goin'. My dreams are far too big to stop now . . ."[7]

Clearly, for Dolly taking risks has always been a matter of faith.

The same is true for you and me.

The Small Screen

In addition to exploring new ways of performing music, Dolly also had the itch to act. And why wouldn't she? As a little towhead singing for an audience of chickens and pigs in the barnyard, Dolly had always loved performing for an audience. She had been doing it her entire life—at church, school, on Cas Walker's programs, on stage at the Grand Ole Opry, and on *The Porter Wagoner Show*.

So it was only natural that a couple years after going solo, she tried hosting her own syndicated TV show, *Dolly!*, which stretched her, but not always in the right direction. I remember her swinging on this huge ivy-covered swing while singing another of her signature hits, "Love Is Like a Butterfly," which had gone to #1 on the country singles charts when it was released in 1974.

Even as my tastes began drifting toward Fleetwood Mac, Elton John, and Bruce Springsteen, I would find Dolly's "Butterfly" fluttering in my head for days. There was something about the way the cascading melody mimicked the delicate, repetitive way a butterfly actually flits and flies, something I was reminded of recently on a trip to Italy when I discovered the Italian word for butterfly, *farfalla*, which has the same lovely cadence.

Unfortunately, even with this infectious signature tune as its theme song (and "I Will Always Love You" closing out each episode), Dolly's first syndicated TV series didn't fly beyond one season. Ratings were high, but the long hours and lack of focus weren't working for her. Looking back, Dolly wondered if the eclectic mix of guests—including Bob Keeshan (Captain Kangaroo) and Anson Williams (Potsie from *Happy Days*)—might have confused viewers unfamiliar with her personality and style.

Even though her first foray with hosting her own TV show didn't go as planned, I love the way Dolly followed her instincts throughout the process. She wasn't afraid to cancel her contract and end the show despite its relative popularity, because she knew it didn't accurately reflect her—her music, her style, and her choice of guests. Although she did host a number of amazing peer performers—Linda Ronstadt, Emmylou Harris, and Kenny Rogers—with whom she formed lifelong bonds of friendship and musical collaboration.

Despite her disappointment with the show, Dolly didn't seem to mind because she had already set her sights much higher—on the big screen. She and her manager had been waiting for the right opportunity for Dolly to break into movies for some time. And when Jane Fonda called with a role in a movie she was producing called *9 to 5*, they knew their patience had paid off. Dolly was about to stretch her wings once again and fly higher than ever before.

The Big Screen

Jane Fonda had already won two Oscars, one for *Klute* (1971) and the other for *Coming Home* (1978), by the time she cast herself, Lily Tomlin, and Dolly in the quintessential working woman comedy. Despite her desire to expand her creative horizons, Dolly didn't consider herself an actress and knew she had to proceed carefully. When Jane Fonda pitched the role of Doralee Rhodes to her, however, Dolly conceded that the character reflected a version of herself that would be easy to play.

As the sexy secretary to the boss (played by Dabney Coleman), Doralee gave Dolly an opportunity to express herself in new comedic ways that also reflected the truth of her experience as a smart, beautiful woman striving to succeed in a male-dominated world. Because of her appearance, along with the lies told by her lustful boss whose advances she consistently rebuffs, Doralee is assumed to be another dumb blonde sleeping her way up the corporate ladder. Once Fonda's character, Judy, and Tomlin's Violet give Doralee a chance, they take matters into their own hands to put their boss in his place once and for all, of course with hilarious results.

Watching the movie now, I found it funnier than I remembered, even if a little stilted and slapstick at times. Overall, though, the film's seemingly exaggerated humor about the serious topics of sexism, sexual harassment, and gender pay equality in the workplace seem even more relevant in the current cultural climate. Despite its humorous treatment of such powerful issues, *9 to 5* brought mainstream awareness front and center in a way that many men would watch and laugh about, especially

Know When to Stretch Your Wings

those dismissive of feminism and oblivious to their own sexist beliefs—men like my father.

Along with starring in the film, Dolly also wrote its theme song of the same name. In yet another display of her musical brilliance, Dolly incorporated the typing tempo that marries the melody to the movie's theme of hardworking women fighting to get ahead. She was inspired by the clicking of her famous acrylic nails while waiting onset, aware of the sound's similarity to the staccato of typewriter keys. The song "9 to 5" became one of Dolly's biggest hits of all time, going to #1 on the Billboard charts for both pop and country before going platinum. Her experience with the film also inspired her to write songs for a Broadway musical version of *9 to 5*.

Dolly Parton, left, Lily Tomlin, center, and Jane Fonda arrive at New York's Sutton Theater, for the premiere of the movie, *9 to 5*.

Dolly's risks paid off and propelled her to new heights of stardom.

She wasn't just a country singer and songwriter.

She wasn't just a pop sensation with a string of hits.

She wasn't just an ensemble actress in a wildly successful comedy film.

She was just Dolly.

Test Your Wings

While you and I may not soar in the same air space as Dolly, we're all given opportunities when we can choose to play it safe and maintain status quo or take a leap of faith and test our wings.

Perhaps I would have made the same decision to change careers without Dolly's example. But seeing her take creative risks—the kind anchored by an awareness of who she is and what she's about—definitely inspired me. And she has influenced countless others to be true to themselves in a variety of areas, both personal and professional. Dolly consistently reminds us to examine our hearts—and to be honest about who we are and what we want—so that we can risk being true to ourselves.

Time after time, Dolly Parton has courageously stepped out in faith and taken risks way outside what's expected of her. Whether it's the hard decision to leave a longtime friend and business partner like Porter Wagoner, the risk to write and record in a variety of musical genres, or the challenge of lighting up the silver screen before millions of moviegoers, Dolly doesn't back down. Even when her risks don't produce the desired results, Dolly uses each one as a learning experience. In a career spanning more than six decades, she has consistently stretched her wings—and she's not through yet!

Divine Dose of Dolly

Those who hope in the LORD
will renew their strength.
They will soar on wings like eagles;
they will run and not grow weary,
they will walk and not be faint.
ISAIAH 40:31

- When have you taken a risk to pursue your dreams? What was the result? What would you do differently if you had it to do over again? Why?
- How do you usually respond when faced with a major life decision? Do you tend to be more objective (logical and fact-based) or more instinctive (emotional and heart-based)?

Listen to Dolly sing "Eagle When She Flies" before answering the following questions. Although she wrote and recorded this song later in her career (1991) than the events covered in this chapter, this song definitely reflects the spirit of risk and resilience we see in all of Dolly's decisions.

Know When to Stretch Your Wings

🦋 How does the song's melody make you feel? Happy, sad, wistful, hopeful, encouraged—something else? How do the lyrics of this song speak to you in the midst of what you're facing in your life right now?

🦋 Did you notice the contrast between being compared to a sparrow during hard times and an eagle soaring above it all? Both of these birds are also featured in well-known Bible verses—check out Matthew 10:29 and Isaiah 40:31 in your favorite version of the Good Book. How do these two references reinforce the theme of this song?

Dear God,

I'm so grateful for all the ways you have blessed me over the years, even during times when I might not have been following you and listening to your voice faithfully. You work through all things, even the mistakes I've made and the painful seasons of my life. Give me the courage to trust you when I'm faced with new opportunities or decisions about my life's direction. Just as I see in the example set by Dolly, help me stay true to the person you created me to be.

Amen.

CHAPTER 4

Love like a Butterfly While Busy as a Bee

Faith, hope, and love are the three most important words in my life. I believe it is faith that helps you achieve those things you hope for and that love is the reason for all of it.
　　　　　DOLLY PARTON

Dolly had just moved from East Tennessee to Music City. With the help of her uncle Bill, she was hard at work, making the rounds at various record companies and performing venues. Nashville was home—just where Dolly needed to be to see her dreams come true.

One day she sat outside the Wishy Washy Laundromat, sipping an RC Cola and waiting on her clothes to dry. Dressed in what she describes as a "rib-tickler" outfit, Dolly caught the attention of a young man driving by. He called out to her, warning her she would probably get sunburned. She smiled and waved, thinking he was just being friendly. Then he turned around and drove by again, pulled in, and began chatting and flirting with the beautiful blonde.

Dolly has often described meeting Carl Dean that day as love at first sight. Not only was he ruggedly Marlboro-man handsome, something about him was different than the boys she had dated back home in Sevierville—something irresistible. For one thing, Carl seemed interested in her mind and personality, not just her sexy body. "I remember looking into his eyes and getting the most wonderful feeling," she said.[1]

Love at the Laundromat

The attraction Dolly felt after laying eyes on the friendly stranger was definitely mutual. Looking back, Dean shared, "My first thought was I'm gonna marry that girl. My second thought was, 'Lord, she's good lookin'."[2] At the time, Dean was twenty-one, three years older than Dolly, and working in his family's asphalt paving business.

Looking for a husband was low on Dolly's list of priorities though. Most of the young men she had dated back home planned to settle down and start a family right away. But Dolly had come to Nashville to be a star, which consumed all her time and energy. She didn't want to get distracted and have her attention divided

Love like a Butterfly While Busy as a Bee

by a serious relationship. Still, she couldn't resist the six-foot-tall man who seemed eager to listen to her talk about her dreams.

She and Carl Dean ended up seeing each other every day the following week.

Because she was babysitting most days, Dolly had to stay close to her apartment building. Carl would come by and hang out with her, the two talking and listening to his portable transistor radio, staying on the front porch or keeping the front door open to reflect their propriety for the benefit of any nosy neighbors. When Dolly finally got a night off, Carl picked her up for their first real date, but didn't tell her where they were going. Instead he drove her to a neighborhood and pulled into the driveway of a private home. Leading her inside, Carl introduced Dolly to his mother and said, "Fix this girl a plate. She's the one I'm going to marry."[3]

Dolly was flabbergasted, to say the least! And she sensed that the new man in her life wasn't joking. With a conflicting cocktail of emotions swirling inside, Dolly somehow managed to get through the evening, clearly intrigued by the quiet confidence and peculiar personality of Carl Dean. As they continued to see each other, Dolly realized she was falling in love with Carl but was worried because he had never expressed his love to her, despite revealing his intention to marry her.

Their romance reached a turning point when Carl announced to Dolly that he had joined the National

Guard and would be going away to boot camp for six weeks. Even more ominous, of course, was the very real possibility that he could be deployed to Vietnam, where the growing conflict had become a war unlike any other. Faced without seeing Carl on a regular if not daily basis and afraid of the dangers ahead if he went overseas, Dolly realized she cared deeply for this man in ways she had not experienced before.

Stationed at Fort Stewart, Georgia, not far from Savannah, Carl asked Dolly to visit him. She agreed, bringing some of her younger siblings as well as her best friend Judy Ogle along to enjoy the beach. In her autobiography Dolly mentions that during this time she had just started experimenting with wigs to create the piled-high bouffant style popular then in the sixties. At the base when she finally saw Carl, Dolly ran up and hugged him so hard that his chin knocked her wig off! She jokes, of course, about "flipping her wig" over him, but the growing love she felt for Carl Dean was no laughing matter.

Once he returned to Nashville, Carl resumed working with his father in their family business, quite a way across town from where Dolly was living at the time. This coincided with her early days of finding work on radio shows hosted by Ralph Emery and Eddie Hill. Thanks to the support and persistence of her uncle Bill, Dolly had just signed with Fred Foster at Monument Records as well. The sparks of her dreams were beginning to catch fire.

While they still managed to see each other most every

day, the busyness and distance began to take its toll. As Dolly recalls what ended up being Carl's backhanded marriage proposal, he told her she either had to move closer to where he lived or they had to get married. She protested that he had never even told her that he loved her, pretty much a deal breaker for any gal. But the stoic, reserved Carl pointed out that she already knew he loved her, which she acknowledged. Nonetheless, Dolly began the process of helping her new fiancé, as well as her father and other male family members, say the actual words, "I love you" without shame, embarrassment, or prompting from others.

Dolly accepted Carl's awkward proposal, but they quickly discovered a major obstacle—her career.

Run to Ringgold

Dolly and Carl hoped to marry as soon as possible. Carl's mother, Ginny Dean, loved Dolly and couldn't wait to plan a big church wedding, especially since her daughter had deprived her that joy by eloping. But when Dolly shared the news of her engagement with Fred Foster, he asked her to postpone her wedding for at least a year while they continued to launch her career. He thought her public image would carry more sex appeal without a new husband standing beside her. Reluctantly, Dolly agreed to wait and broke the news to Carl and Mama Dean.

After talking it over, though, Dolly and Carl decided

they couldn't wait an entire year and planned to marry in secret out of state, where it wouldn't be reported in Tennessee. They chose Ringgold, Georgia, just across the state line below Chattanooga, which coincidentally is where my parents also got married. Apparently, Ringgold had become a kind of mini-Vegas, and lots of couples went there to elope.

Dolly had promised her own mother that she would never get married without Mama Parton being there, so Avie Lee accompanied the happy couple on their drive down to Georgia. Getting their marriage license proved easy, but standing before the justice of the peace in city hall, Dolly couldn't go through with it. As much as she wanted to be Carl's wife, she needed their wedding to be at least a little more special.

Dolly wanted to be married in a church, but that would mean finding one and waiting at least another day or two. Nonetheless, that's what they did. Pastor Don Duvall at Ringgold Baptist Church married Carl Thomas Dean and Dolly Rebecca Parton two days later with his wife and Mrs. Parton in attendance as witnesses. The happy couple drove home, legally man and wife at last, but with only a few hours to spend together before they both had to be at work early the next morning.

Dolly had found the love of her life. She knew, however, that her marriage to Carl would not conform to everyone else's expectations. Like so many aspects of her life, Dolly created her own way, making sure her new husband understood the importance of her dreams and the hard work required for them to come true.

There would be weeks when they wouldn't see each other as she toured, performed, and promoted her career. She would not be a traditional, stay-at-home wife there to fix his lunch or cook his supper each day. And even though they both knew their relationship would be tested, I wonder if that happy couple returning from Ringgold ever imagined the trials to come—or the public scrutiny they would face.

Like anything worth having, their love would be tested.

The Love of My Life

I met my love, not at the laundromat, but in a school cafeteria in West Knoxville, where a new church had just been started. I had just graduated from UT and was in my first year of a graduate program, working as a teaching assistant. I had already burned out from the party scene while an undergraduate, culminating in a major shift by the time I finished my undergraduate degree.

I realized that all my drinking, partying, and sleeping around was an attempt to run away from some things in my life I needed to face. This led me to commit my life to God wholeheartedly, desiring a much deeper faith than I had planted by joining the Baptist church in childhood. As a result, many of my friends were Christians, and instead of hitting the bars, clubs, or frat houses on weekends, I was usually in the library or a local church.

I had also started seeing a counselor, stopped drinking entirely, and committed to a year of celibacy after several years of sowing wild oats. While it was painful dealing with some issues from childhood, I liked facing my life head-on and looking to a brighter future. I was committed to getting my act together and no longer running from the issues I carried inside. My faith was a vital part of this season of growth.

Fellowship Church was small, with only about sixty people, mostly college students and young families. The pastor was a young dynamic guy with a brilliant mind and a big heart. Our services were casual but focused, and I liked that I had to interact with other people beyond the anonymous handshakes and smiles of the large established churches I had visited. Naturally, the young single adults gravitated toward one another, about a dozen of us, a few looking for love interests perhaps, but most of us just looking for new friends and kindred spirits.

After a few weeks, someone offered to host our little group in their home, just a relaxed time to enjoy a meal together and get better acquainted. There I enjoyed meeting a few new faces as well as having an extended conversation with others I'd already met. While standing and chatting, I felt someone back into me, and I automatically turned. A beautiful brunette woman with the most piercing, translucent blue-green eyes I'd ever seen was turning around at the same time and looking back at me. Realizing we had backed into one another, we smiled and politely apologized, but didn't introduce ourselves.

Over the following weeks, I learned this woman's name was Dotti, actually Dorothy after her grandmother, and that she too was a grad student at UT. She had a maturity about her, was clearly intelligent, and had a quirky yet classy style in the way she dressed. With thick, dark brown hair she wore at shoulder length and those amazing eyes, I found her incredibly attractive. But I had promised myself not to date anyone during my year of clean living, the only way I knew to avoid temptation before it started.

So as Dotti and I began to talk regularly at church, I thought of her only as a friend. She was completing a master's degree in counseling and social work, was a native Knoxvillian, and worked at her family's business designing and equipping restaurants. She read voraciously, loved poetry, listened to "Prairie Home Companion," and had an eye for beauty, as evidenced by frequent trips to Carolina beaches and the stained-glass window she'd rescued from a salvage yard to hang in her apartment.

One Sunday after church she asked if I wanted to have lunch, and I quickly agreed, eager to continue our conversation about writers we loved and to postpone the essay I needed to write. We ate barbeque at a place not far from the river and then went for a walk. Dotti was unlike the girls I had dated in college, mostly sorority types I'd met at parties.

Dotti was an adult, had been engaged twice but never married, and wasn't in a hurry to find out if the third time was indeed the charm. That Sunday afternoon I found myself telling her my story, revealing things about my family and upbringing I hadn't told anyone. She was such a great listener, so engaged and receptive, that once I got started, I couldn't stop pouring my heart out.

I left our time together that afternoon with my heart lighter. I liked the freedom of not thinking about her romantically and just enjoying the profound connection we seemed to share. I knew I probably would not have told her half the personal stuff I'd rambled on about if I wanted to impress her and ask her out. But I felt like I could be real with her in a way I'd never experienced before. I liked her immensely and had experienced firsthand her gift for listening and offering wise counsel and encouragement.

I had made a new friend and that was all.
Right.

Confirmation from Dolly

Fast-forward five months. It's an unseasonably warm autumn night in November. Dotti and I have driven up to Sevierville for dinner at a famed five-star restaurant. We're celebrating my birthday as well as just having some special time together before the holidays roll in. We've been officially a couple for about eight weeks, right after she returned from a beach vacation with several girlfriends at the end of August. With my one year of good behavior completed, I didn't rush to ask her out, but we quickly drifted into patterns of talking each day and seeing each other when we could.

We've each come clean with each other. I learned that Dotti wanted to go out with me and kept attending church and university events in hopes of running into me. It actually became a comedy of errors because almost every time she attended a choir practice, small group meeting, or poetry reading where I had planned to be, something came up. So she quit trying so hard and decided to forget about me while she enjoyed her two-week vacation in Hilton Head with three of her closest friends.

Only as soon as she left town, I couldn't get her off my mind. We had agreed not to phone each day and to just talk after she returned. But her absence sent me into a panic. I hadn't realized how much I had come to enjoy her, rely on her, and care about her until she wasn't there. While she was away, I realized that I loved her and wanted to marry her—which was crazy because, like Dolly, I had planned to put my career first and not worry about marrying and settling down for at least five or six years.

But I had this nagging sense that if I didn't marry this amazing, beautiful, extraordinary woman, I would be missing out on one of the greatest blessings of my life. So I told our pastor, the same young guy at our little church, which was now not so little anymore. He questioned me, testing to see if it was just infatuation or the resurrected physical desire of a young man who'd abstained for the past year. But I must have passed his test because he told me to keep praying about it, and if I felt the same way when Dotti returned from vacation, then I ought to tell her my intentions.

Which is exactly what I did, only it didn't quite go as planned. Dotti called to let me know she was back in Knoxville and to invite me over for dinner. When I got there, she looked tanned and rested, happy to see me but also perhaps a bit wary. After hugging me and pouring me a glass of sweet tea, she said, "Oh, I brought you something from the beach." Without waiting to see her gift, I jumped right in, "I've been thinking a lot while you were away, and I realized I'm in love with you and I want to marry you. I'm not sure when I'll pop the question but that's where I'm headed."

Talk about speechless! It's a wonder I didn't scare her off right then and there. She just looked at me for the longest time, trying to figure out if I was joking or if I could possibly be serious about this life-changing profession I'd just made. "Okay," she said, after she must have decided I was sincere. "Thank you for telling me. I'm going to need a little time to process everything. And in the meantime, just be patient and keep letting me know what you're thinking about where our relationship is going."

Love like a Butterfly While Busy as a Bee

Which I promised to do, which in turn brings me back to Sevierville, Tennessee, about a block from the Sevier County Courthouse on a warm November evening. By this point we had both told each other those words Carl Dean found so hard to say out loud, "I love you." I had also gathered that Dotti was expecting me to propose to her at Christmas, which made perfect sense because we'd be seeing both our families and friends visiting from out of town.

Only, I have never liked to be predictable. So I had moved up the timetable. I had already met her parents and had asked their blessing to marry their daughter. They had agreed, politely and perhaps a bit hesitantly. I had purchased an engagement ring at an antique jewelry store specializing in vintage pieces: a solitaire one-carat Ceylon sapphire the same color as Dotti's eyes, set in platinum, circa 1920. I was about to burst inside, but tried to play it cool and just enjoy our dinner like it was no big deal.

Because the weather was so mild, after dinner we strolled down the street toward the old courthouse building, just enjoying the quiet love between us. That's when we saw Dolly—well, the recently erected bronze statue of her, sitting on a big old boulder in front of the courthouse, strumming her guitar. Crafted by famed Southern artist Jim Gray, an acclaimed painter as well as sculptor, the larger-than-life tribute features a dedication plaque reading, "This statue of Dolly Parton was erected through the generosity of the people of Sevier County, Dedicated May 3, 1987."[4]

The Faith of Dolly Parton

Bronze statue of Dolly in front of the courthouse in Sieverville

We both remembered hearing about the statue's dedication a couple years earlier, shortly after Dollywood had opened, but neither of us had seen it. I explained to Dotti my admiration and appreciation for Dolly and wondered what my future wife would think about my display of the kind of devotion usually reserved for tween girls and their favorite boy bands. But I needn't have worried because Dotti already loved Dolly almost as much as I did. As a teenager Dotti had even worked selling concessions at Silver Dollar City, the nearby amusement park that became a foundational piece of Dollywood.

Seeing Dolly's statue that evening seemed like one of the best confirmations I could've hoped for. I felt like she was sort of smiling down on us, blessing us with a knowing look, sending us on our way toward a new life together as man and wife. I waited until we were back at Dotti's apartment to get down on one knee and ask her to be my wife. She didn't hesitate to accept my proposal and make me the happiest man on earth. Later, my bride-to-be told me that she had said a little prayer while we were lingering there in front of Dolly's statue, asking God to give us the kind of love that would last a lifetime.

Going the Distance

In describing her relationship with her husband, Dolly has consistently commented on how different—even opposite—their personalities are from one another. While Dolly is bubbly and outgoing, Carl is reserved and shy. Dolly loves being around people and draws energy from others; Carl likes being alone and needs time to himself to recharge. Dolly communicates in a direct, no-nonsense style, comfortably transparent with other people. She has described Carl, on the other hand, as being odd, mysterious, and very private.

But there's plenty Dolly and Carl have in common: dedication to family, a strong work ethic, an enjoyment of life's simple pleasures, a lifelong curiosity to learn, and a playful sense of humor. Most of all, they clearly share core values about what it means to love each other and remain committed to one another throughout life's ups and downs. She knows it's hard enough for any two people to sustain their love over a lifetime, let alone with added pressures caused by fame, frequent travel, and public scrutiny.

Commitment, communication, and character sustain their strong relationship. Honesty and trust are paramount. "It's the way I am wired, so I will always be honest, and I expect the same thing in return," explains Dolly, stressing that she means "dead-on, wide-eyed, blunt, total, transparent honesty."[5]

This kind of love also includes a willingness to accept each other and appreciate one another's differences. Early on, Carl made it clear that he would never be comfortable being "Mr. Parton," the kind of Hollywood husband who enjoys basking in the glow of his superstar spouse's success. Dolly relates how Carl accompanied her to her first major awards event when a song she and Uncle Bill had written, "Put It Off Until Tomorrow," was named BMI's song of the year in 1966.

Love like a Butterfly While Busy as a Bee

They rented a tux for Carl to wear, and he patiently endured a long night full of fans, photographers, reporters, industry insiders, and other stars. When they got home, Carl reiterated his love and support for Dolly and her pursuit of stardom, but made it clear that he didn't enjoy the kind of event they had attended that night. If it was okay with her, Carl preferred to stay home. Dolly agreed, realizing the importance of respecting this significant difference.

While Dolly has recorded dozens of studio albums, toured around the world, filmed movies in Hollywood, hosted TV series and specials and produced others, Carl has kept the home fires burning. He's been more than content to continue working at his asphalt paving business, enjoying a good-old-boy lifestyle that would make my daddy proud. He's frugal and likes to stick close to home, enjoying time at the lake and traveling in their RV.

While he has seldom had his picture taken or attended Dolly's concerts, Carl Dean enjoys fixing things around the house, puttering in his workshop, going to ball games and races, and looking for "treasures" in junk yards and flea markets. According to Dolly, her husband is also a gifted poet, artist, and comedian, inventing characters and monologues to perform for her and close friends. Overall, he sounds like quite a character, a man confident in his own abilities and comfortable in his own skin—a private, faithful man's man who happened to fall in love with one of the biggest stars of all time.

What a joy it must have been for them both to have celebrated their golden anniversary by renewing their vows in 2016. "I wouldn't trade the last fifty years for nothin' on earth," Carl said at the time, while Dolly indicated she would gladly make the same choice if she had it to do all over again.[6] Any couple who remains committed to one another after five decades of living life together surely knows something about what it means to love!

Loving Others Well

In addition to loving her husband throughout her lifetime, Dolly has faithfully loved her family, close friends, and team members with the same fierce devotion. Her lifelong best friend Judy Ogle has been with Dolly since growing up together in the hollers of the Smoky Mountains. I suspect Dolly values having someone who understands where she started who has also accompanied her during her ascent to stardom, someone other than a Parton sibling.

While Dolly is quick to point out that neither of them is perfect, she also credits Judy's dedication, unwavering loyalty, and shared passion for enjoying life as keys to her success. "We have had our problems, our ups and downs, but the love has always been great enough to overcome."[7] Their relationship reflects the biblical truth that a friend loves at all times (Proverbs 17:17). Judy works just as hard as Dolly, being both her boss and best friend, and remains incredibly protective. She rarely gives interviews

Love like a Butterfly While Busy as a Bee

or makes public statements, valuing her own privacy as much as Dolly's.

Dolly thinks of Judy like a sister, and in fact is the only person who gets to call Judy "Sissy" because she's a part of the family. The two of them have had many adventures together, some with hilarious results as Dolly has often shared in interviews, from getting lost in New York City to daring each other to streak through Beverly Hills. They share a mischievous sense of humor and enjoy playing practical jokes and pulling pranks. But they have also enjoyed going on spiritual retreats together, discussing the Bible and all that's going on in their lives. "If she has a problem, I can usually find a scripture that will be of some help," says Dolly.[8]

Judy Ogle is not the only friend and team member Dolly credits for her success. Any time Dolly talks about her life, she is quick to give credit to the people who have faithfully supported her along the way, particularly Don Warden. Dolly met Don, one of the best steel guitar players in the business as well as a savvy businessman, in 1967 after she joined *The Porter Wagoner Show*. Dolly hit it off with Don and his wife, Ann, and when Dolly left the show, Don left also and worked with Dolly for the rest of his career.

She soon called him "Mr. Everything" because of his gift for problem solving, making great decisions, and appreciating Dolly more as a friend than a business asset. When Don passed away just shy of his eighty-eighth birthday in 2017, Dolly said, "He was like a father, a brother, a partner and one of my best friends. I feel like a piece of my heart is missing today. Certainly a huge piece of my life is gone. Rest in peace Don and know for sure that I will always love you."[9]

In addition to these two pillars, Judy and Don, Dolly often mentions her gratitude for team members Teresa Hughes, Richard Dennison, and Ted Miller, as well as many others. Reading through over a hundred articles and interviews, as well as Dolly's two books, I was struck by how often she names others and gives them credit for all they do for her. It's refreshing to hear a star, especially someone as larger-than-life as Dolly, consistently make sure that her fans know that it takes a hardworking, dedicated team to achieve the results she has accomplished over her lifetime. "I truly love all my closest colleagues, because I trust them and respect them," Dolly explains. "These folks feel like my family. I will do anything for them, and they will do anything for me."[10]

Through her words but also through her actions, Dolly's definition of love emerges. She has never pretended that relationships of any kind—with Carl, her family, Judy, her band, or other team members—are easy. She has repeatedly emphasized the importance of absolute honesty and open communication. Even if she doesn't like what someone else tells her, Dolly would rather hear the truth than what others think will please her. Clearly, respect for one another and trust are foundational. Loyalty is part of the mix, along with shared values and common goals.

Dolly knows that love is a two-way street. She has never let her stardom keep her from giving to others as much as she receives from them. She manages the tension between devotion to others and the pursuit of one's goals—a friction virtually everyone feels at times—with grace and poise. Even while busy as a bee, she makes loving others look easy and natural, a beautiful butterfly leaving joy in its path.

Love Never Fails

Yes, if there's a secret to Dolly's success, it has to be love. She not only loves what she does and loves her fans, but she simply loves people. Despite tabloid speculation and public curiosity about her private life and personal relationships, the fact remains that Dolly has remained married to her husband, Carl Dean, for over fifty years. She has been a best friend to Judy Ogle and worked closely with many of the same people throughout her decades-long career. Dolly has also loved her family and worked hard to include them in her success, which we'll explore in chapter seven.

I'm not sure there's any better example of her faith in action than the way she loves others. The Bible tells us, "Dear friends, let us love one another, for love comes from God. Everyone who loves has been born of God and knows God" (1 John 4:7). Dolly credits her love of God as the anchor of her life. She begins each day with him and tries to reflect his love in all she does.

As successful as she's been throughout most of her career, Dolly could have lived a life stereotypical of so many other stars—a half-dozen marriages and divorces, numerous affairs and scandals, an estranged family, and no real friends. People with fame and a lot of money haven't always been the most caring people. Instead, Dolly has shown the world what it looks like, whether in the early days when she had nothing or now at the stratospheric top, to never lose sight of what it means to love.

Dolly is living proof that love never fails.

Divine Dose of Dolly

Above all, love each other deeply, because love covers over a multitude of sins.
1 PETER 4:8

- In one of her most famous love songs, Dolly compares love to a butterfly, noting that both are rare and gentle. What animal, insect, or living creature would you use as a metaphor for your view of love? Why?
- Dolly has often credited the success of her marriage to Carl Dean to their willingness to accept and appreciate each other's differences without trying to change them. Do you agree that loving someone means accepting them without wanting them to change in some way? Why or why not?

So many of Dolly's hits are love songs or deal with some aspect of love. If you have a favorite of hers that focuses on love, feel free to listen to it before answering the following questions. Otherwise, listen to Dolly sing "Think About Love" before considering your responses.

- How does knowing Dolly's commitment to her husband, Carl Dean, has lasted more than fifty years influence the way you experience this love song? Why?
- Who comes to mind in your own life when you hear this love song? Who are the people you have loved the most throughout your life? If you could add a verse to this song to express what your spouse or loved ones mean to you, what would you say?

Dear God,

You are the source of all love. I am only able to love others because you have first loved me. Help me to give as much as I receive in all my relationships and to balance my commitments to my loved ones with the pursuit of the purpose you have given me. Let all that I do be done in love. Thank you for loving me so much!

Amen.

CHAPTER 5

Practice More Than You Preach

I have always said that if God gave me success, I would do my best to share the gifts that he has blessed me with.
   DOLLY PARTON

Dolly hasn't always considered herself a Christian—at least, not a perfect one.

Shortly after leaving Porter and branching out on her own, Dolly described her faith to one writer by making an important distinction: "My religious beliefs are very, very strong. I would like to think that I have a Christian outlook on life as far as the way I treat people. Still, I know the Bible says you must believe and be baptized—and I do believe in God and I have been baptized—but I don't consider myself a Christian."[1]

While it might sound shocking at first, Dolly goes on

to explain, "I feel like God and me have always been good friends. I'm just totally aware of Him. I feel He helps me even though I am a sinner. I know that He's never left me. I know that I count on Him, and I know I depend on Him. I feel like I owe my success so much to that, because nothin' good ever happens to me that I don't remember to thank God for that happenin' to me. Nothin' bad ever happens to me that I don't remember to ask God to help me out of it."[2]

This tension is reflected in one of Dolly's most overtly spiritual songs, "The Seeker," which casts the narrator as a "poor sinful creature" as well as a broken vessel, someone struggling with her own weaknesses, asking the Lord to guide her and keep her. What's clear in the lyrics of this song, as well as that early interview and others, is that Dolly never wanted to appear self-righteous, holier-than-thou, or spiritually perfect in any way.

To avoid being a hypocrite, saying one thing and doing another, Dolly actually reveals her faith to be *very* Christian. She acknowledges her sinfulness and her reliance on God. She speaks with humility and, over the years, with the mature wisdom that comes from living by faith and relying on grace. Most of all, she demonstrates the kind of love in action modeled by Jesus during his time on earth, one characterized by generosity, forgiveness, and compassion for all people. Dolly said, "I learned a long time ago that 'telling' or 'preaching' to young people—or adults, for that matter—just bounces off their ears like a satellite. They don't catch it; they just deflect it away."³

What people catch, however, is what they see someone do.

Giving and Forgiving

Dolly Parton is all for giving and forgiving.

When it comes to faith, it's easy to talk the talk but much harder to walk what you talk. From the early days of her career, though, Dolly has consistently practiced more than she's preached. For as much as she's talked about her faith and relationship with God, Dolly has never used her spiritual beliefs to condemn, rebuke, or proselytize others, at least to my knowledge. In fact, she points out, "If people want to pass judgment, they're already sinning. The sin of judging is just as bad as any other sin they might say somebody else is committing. I try to love everybody."⁴

Instead she has practiced unconditional kindness and compassion, respecting and welcoming all people, and taking the high road when facing conflicts and problems—including lawsuits.

You can criticize the way she dresses or decide you don't care for her musical style or the sound of her voice. You can question her lifestyle or the decisions she has made throughout her career. You can find fault with the way she lives out her faith in comparison to your own or others. But you can't deny the unwavering generosity—both material and spiritual—of Dolly Parton.

From an early age, she reflects the Bible's emphasis on exercising what you believe and not just nodding in agreement when a preacher's talking. The Bible stresses, "Do not merely listen to the word, and so deceive yourselves. Do what it says" (James 1:22). Jesus even made a startling contrast between someone who hears his words and practices them versus someone who lets the truth go in one ear and out the other:

> Therefore everyone who hears these words of mine and puts them into practice is like a wise man who built his house on the rock. The rain came down, the streams rose, and the winds blew and beat against that house; yet it did not fall, because it had its foundation on the rock. But everyone who hears these words of mine and does not put them into practice is like a foolish man who built his house on sand. The rain came down, the streams rose, and the winds blew and beat against that house, and it fell with a great crash.
>
> *Matthew 7:24–27*

Others might disagree, but I find Dolly's bedrock faith to be as solid as her beloved Smoky Mountains. In fact, a quick click to the website for the Great Smoky Mountains National Park informs me that the Smokies are composed of sedimentary rock formed by clay, silt, sand,

and gravel. "As more and more of these sediments were deposited, they were eventually cemented together and changed into layers of rock over nine miles thick."[5] This little geology lesson fits perfectly within Jesus's metaphor because Dolly's faith has accumulated over her lifetime from countless acts of selfless giving, cementing her legacy as a humanitarian and philanthropist.

Always Giving

Dolly's generosity began at an early age. After winning the $250 prize for climbing to the top of Cas Walker's greased pole when she was a kid, Dolly used it to buy her family a new TV. Unfortunately, her purchase proved so popular with family, friends, and neighbors that her parents couldn't go to sleep each night without a small crowd lingering to watch the hypnotic sights and sounds of the little electronic box—even after stations signed off! While the TV had to go, I suspect Dolly found other ways to help her family with her prize money.

And it wasn't just her family that Dolly was committed to helping. Even in the early days of her career after joining Porter Wagoner's show, she was eager to help everyone back home. The result was the first annual "Dolly Day" in Sevierville, Tennessee, back in 1970. Only six years after graduating from the Sevier County High School, Dolly was back in her old alma mater's gymnasium, recording her first live album, "A Real Live Dolly." She credits Porter with guiding and inspiring her in this idea. "He insisted that the event be produced as a live album, and he arranged for many well known Nashville musicians to be a part of it. The album was a success and it made me very proud."[6]

Please understand that this wasn't just an opportunity for self-promotion. In the spirit of giving, Dolly "announced she was donating her part of the proceeds of that night's show to set up a scholarship fund for deserving students at the high school. She promised to return for benefit shows whenever they were needed to maintain the fund."[7] Needless to say, Dolly has more than kept that promise. According to the current Dollywood Foundation website, at least five scholarships help students from the area attend the college of their choice.

Charity Begins at Home

For Dolly, charity always begins at home. She has done more than simply make her friends, family, and neighbors proud—she's brought in jobs, dollars, tourists, books, grants, and scholarships. She launched Dollywood in 1986—a theme park celebrating the heritage of the Smoky Mountains that provides jobs for several thousand people in the area. In the process she's become an ambassador not only for her hometown but also for Tennessee, appropriately known as the Volunteer State.

In recent years, Dolly has led the effort to help more than a thousand families in Sevier County who lost their homes due to devastating fires in 2016. Through her foundation she created the My People Fund through which she distributed one thousand dollars per month for six months to each family that lost their primary residence. After the completion of the initial distribution, over $400 *million* has been raised and given to those who lost their homes, including scholarships for high school seniors from those families.

Dolly saw a need, knew something had to be done, and didn't wait on anyone else to do it. She jumped in, raising money and distributing much needed resources, including cash, to people who suddenly found themselves homeless. She didn't have to do it. It would have been so easy to think other agencies and programs would help those poor souls who lost everything. But Dolly embodies one of my favorite Bible stories: the tale of the Good Samaritan.

The Good Samaritan

Once a man from Detroit was driving through the Smoky Mountains on his way to Atlanta. He got lost on a back road and before he knew it, some rednecks carjacked him, beat him, stripped him, and left him for dead in the middle of nowhere. Soon a country preacher came along, but when he saw the man lying in the ditch, he kept on going. A little while later, a deacon from the little church down in the holler drove up, saw the unconscious man on the side of the road, and passed by in a cloud of dust.

Then the town tramp happened to drive by in her red Cadillac, saw the man, braked to a stop, and knew she had to do something. With no cell reception up in the mountains, the woman took some Watkins salve and an old blanket and bandaged the man as best she could. She dragged him into the passenger seat of her car and drove him to a little bed-and-breakfast nearby. There she paid for a room, left extra money with the hostess, and said, "Take care of him. I'll be back soon to check on him and pay you for your time and trouble."

I have no idea how Dolly would retell the parable of the Good Samaritan, but it's fun to imagine. Jesus told this famous tale in response to a question from a man identified as "an expert in the law" who wanted to test Jesus (Luke 10:25). The man asks Christ what he has to do in order to receive eternal life, to which Jesus replied: "'Love the Lord your God with all your heart and with all your soul and with all your strength and with all your mind'; and, 'Love your neighbor as yourself'" (Luke 10:27).

Not content to accept Jesus's answer, and because he wanted to justify himself, the law expert pressed in by asking, "Who is my neighbor?" (Luke 10:29). And that's when the man got more than he bargained for, I suspect, because Jesus told the story about a man traveling from Jerusalem to Jericho who's robbed, stripped, beaten, and left for dead. A priest passes by and ignores the man. As does a Levite, a member of a prestigious Jewish tribe who often served in the temple. But it's the Samaritan—a

Practice More Than You Preach

foreigner most Jews at that time despised—who stops and helps the man, going out of his way to nurse his wounds, take him to a local inn, and arrange for the man's care there (Luke 10:30–35).

Now it would be like shooting fish in a barrel to take potshots at prominent religious leaders today, which might be better contemporary equivalents of priests and Levites, for the ways they ignore the poor, the homeless, the hungry, and disenfranchised in order to focus on their next campus expansion, world tour, jet purchase, or TV broadcast. Not that there's anything wrong with any of those—the Lord truly works in mysterious ways! But I do worry, and perhaps you do too, that we're all tempted to be priests and Levites, far too busy with our own lives and its urgent demands to stop and lend a hand to those in need.

It's also important to note that in Jesus's story it's a Samaritan who finally stops and cares for the man robbed and left to die by the side of the road. At the time Jesus was telling this story, most Jewish people thought Samaritans were beneath them, a nondevout ethnic group resulting from cross-cultural unions with Gentiles, which would have been abhorrent to the Jews. So the fact that Jesus made the hero of this story a Samaritan, someone his audience (especially the law expert quizzing him) would find contemptible, is striking. Sometimes we can get so busy being "religious" that we forget to love people and show them what God's love looks like in action.

Each of us matters to God. And we should care for

other humans, knowing each of us is a child of God. We can get so consumed with putting ourselves and our views first that we don't listen to others, let alone empathize or reach out and help them. A few years ago, the University of Michigan reported its findings from a comprehensive study of prevailing attitudes among college students over thirty years from 1979 to 2009. In those three decades, researchers observed a drastic decline in empathy. Basically, they found people today care about others forty percent less than people did during the 1980s.[8]

It's difficult to identify the various factors contributing to this desensitization. Part of it may be the narcissistic result of living online through social media. Another variable may be the increased exposure of more and more worthy causes competing for visibility and resources. There are so many needs, so many hurting people, so many diseases and disasters, that we become a little calloused. Besides, we've got our own problems and struggles to deal with.

Jesus, however, reminds us through his story of the Good Samaritan that no matter how different we may be, we're all neighbors. We're all given the privilege to help each other, regardless of how much or how little we may have. Jesus wasn't born in a palace to a rich family. He didn't come to command an army for his own political power. He never started a church, launched a building campaign, or showed favoritism to the elite.

Instead, he lived simply and humbly, hanging out with

fishermen and prostitutes, tax collectors and Samaritans, the diseased and disfigured—real people with real needs. Jesus healed them, fed them, forgave them, saved them, and loved them. He turned the religious establishment upside down and revealed his Father's tender heart toward all people.

Cheerful Giving

Dolly has her faults like we all do. But I find more in her example that motivates me to give, to share, and to help others than I see in most celebrities and public figures. And one of the things I love most about Dolly's generosity is that no one even knows the full extent of it. Jesus advised, "When you give to the needy, do not let your left hand know what your right hand is doing" (Matthew 6:3). When you're trying to increase visibility and raise funds for a cause that's important to you, it's tough if you can't talk about it. But there's a difference between using one's celebrity for a cause versus using that cause to expand one's celebrity. But Dolly knows the difference and shows it.

Or rather, she doesn't show it, because for every time she promotes causes near and dear to her heart, such as her Imagination Library (all about that in chapter ten) and the My People Fund, I suspect there are dozens that no one knows about except her and the Good Lord. It took a little digging, but I discovered a variety of causes, nonprofits, hospitals, scholarships, and charities to which Dolly has contributed, in addition to ones operating through the Dollywood Foundation.

These range from donating autographed, personal memorabilia for fund-raisers and charity auctions to giving millions to organizations such as the Make-A-Wish Foundation, the United Way, the Opry Trust Fund, the Save The Music Foundation, the Barbara Davis Center for Childhood Diabetes, as well as numerous schools and hospitals, like the W. O. Smith Music School in Nashville or the Fort Sanders Medical Center in Knoxville.[9] As her longtime friend and fellow icon Kenny Rogers once observed, "I am impressed that Dolly doesn't do anything that doesn't grow to have a widespread impact—it may start locally, but because of her focus and determination, whatever it may be grows to have influence in a much larger way."[10]

Dolly is without a doubt one of the most successful superstars of all time, with an estimated net worth in the hundreds of millions of dollars. While you'll frequently hear her joke about all the money she makes, you won't hear her brag about it or read about her spending it on over-the-top indulgences. Instead, you're likely to see her asking you to partner with a cause she really cares about or to read about some group or person or cause she's helped. If there were only a handful of examples every few years, it would be admirable. But Dolly gives because it's part of who she is. It's part of the way she lives out her faith every day, a sparkling Good Samaritan in spangles and sequins.

Practice More Than You Preach

Dolly signs an autograph for a fan before a performance, 1977.

While Dolly has inspired me to give of my time, talents, and treasure, I know that my donations and contributions are nowhere close to the generosity visible in her life. But giving is not about comparing or competing, as I'm guessing Dolly would be one of the first to remind us. Generosity is an attitude of the heart, a willingness to give of who you are and what you have.

By her example, and of course the one set for all of us by Jesus, Dolly reminds us to take our eyes off of ourselves, if even for a moment, and notice the needs of others. As the Bible explains, "Each of you should give what you have decided in your heart to give, not reluctantly or under compulsion, for God loves a cheerful giver" (2 Corinthians 9:7).

I don't think you can find a more cheerful giver than Dolly Parton!

Forgive One Another

In addition to being *for* giving, Dolly is also *forgiving*. If grace and forgiveness reflect the heart of God, then she has shown us, repeatedly and consistently, how to live by faith and to show God's love to others, especially those who have hurt her, betrayed her, or harmed her. The Bible tells us, "Bear with each other and forgive one another if any of you has a grievance against someone. Forgive as the Lord forgave you" (Colossians 3:13). I see Dolly exercising this kind of forgiveness in one of her most famous, and bittersweet, relationships.

With very different leadership styles and visions for their then-entwined careers, Porter Wagoner and Dolly Parton naturally struggled like any pair of talented, smart, stubborn business partners. When Dolly chose to break away on her own, she knew it would be one of the hardest, most painful decisions of her career. Despite her frustration and anger toward Porter, she cared for him deeply. Which explains why she chose to convey her decision to her friend and mentor the best way she knew how—through a song.

That song, "I Will Always Love You," no doubt touched Porter and brought tears to his eyes. He also knew, aside from its personal message, the song would be a big hit, so he asked Dolly to let him produce it. She agreed. The song, written and performed by Dolly and produced by Porter, peaked at #1 on the country chart. Whether it was professional jealousy or some other reason, five years

Practice More Than You Preach

later Porter sued her for $3 million and a percentage of all her future earnings, claiming that he was responsible for making her a star. Dolly recounts that she experienced the news "like a pan of cold dishwater thrown in my face."[11]

They ended up settling out of court for an undisclosed amount at the time, but which Porter and then later Dolly both acknowledged was around $1 million. While her career was growing by leaps and bounds, Dolly said it wasn't easy coming up with the money for this settlement. She simply didn't have that kind of cash lying around and therefore had to scrape it together, depleting all she and Carl had at the time. "I paid the debt. It took everything I had, everything Carl had, everything I could make for years to come, but I paid it."[12]

Now I don't know about you, but if someone who was a former close friend and business partner treated me this way, I'm not sure I would ever want to hear their name again, let alone speak to them—or perform with them! But Dolly doesn't hold grudges, at least not with Porter. As part of her variety TV series for ABC in the late eighties, Dolly reunited with Porter and his band the Wagonmasters. Consummate professionals during their cheerful banter and performance together, the two seemed to have agreed to let bygones be bygones. Still, I can't imagine it was easy for either of them.

I suspect, however, the two must have forgiven each other by the time Porter was inducted into the Country Music Hall of Fame in 2002, ironically three years after

Dolly had already been inducted. Prior to that ceremony, Dolly wrote in her autobiography, "Porter and I have outlived a lot of the hurt and bitterness we both felt and can once again share a stage from time to time when we work together. So, thank you, Porter Wagoner, for all the good that you have brought to me and forgive me for the bad, as I have forgiven you."[13]

Dolly's forgiveness of Porter Wagoner extended beyond their professional relationship, however. She was there, along with his adult children and family, at his bedside when he passed away October 28, 2007. In an interview the following year, Dolly revealed, "I was with Porter the day he died. We sang and we cried and I sat and held Porter's hand. I had my hand on his heart 'cause it was just flyin'. I knew it wasn't long. He died at 8 that night. It was like losin' a piece of me, like losin' your daddy."[14]

Dolly's love seems to have been greater and more precious to her than any past hurt.

Forgiveness Takes Time

From my experience, forgiveness is a process—even if you agree to it with your head, it's not something you can do easily or efficiently. And it definitely requires faith. There is no greater way to practice your faith than to forgive someone who has broken your heart. This process can be particularly challenging when dealing with family, especially your mother and father.

Practice More Than You Preach

Few people would disagree that relationships with parents are complicated. Once you're an adult, you begin to see your parents as people and not just as your mama and daddy. You recognize their flaws and weaknesses and wonder about their dreams and the particular decisions they made, often because you're facing some of the same choices yourself. Growing up, I didn't always get along with my father or feel like he and I understood each other. I resented caring for him as an alcoholic at the expense of my childhood.

But as I got older, married, and had children of my own, I was shocked at not one but two miracles in my father's life. The first was his sobriety. A lifelong alcoholic who had been drinking moonshine and whiskey since boyhood, my father up and decided to quit drinking in his late fifties. I suspect the aches and pains of middle age were compounded by all the hard living he had done. I'm guessing my father was also starting to think about his own mortality and how to extend his life. Maybe it was neither of those or no reason at all, but one day he just up and quit cold turkey, and for the last dozen years of his life my father never touched a drop of alcohol.

Miracle number two: my father came to know the Lord, accepted Jesus as his Savior, and joined a local church. For a man who had criticized most of the Christians he knew as hypocrites and dismissed the church as yet another attempt to take money out of his pocket, my father might as well have told me he had joined NASA and planned to fly to the moon. Instead he asked me what I thought about baptism, and if I'd be willing to fly from Colorado back to Tennessee to be there for his.

He and my mother were already model grandparents, doting on our three kids in that lavish, giddy way only Papa and Granny can. That my mother enjoyed being with my kids didn't surprise me. But I remember watching my father sit at tea parties with my two preschool-age daughters, asking for more apple juice and then talking to their American Girl dolls as if they would answer back. I remember seeing him lie on the floor with my toddler son lining up Matchbox cars for their next race. I even felt angry, resentful that he could be so engaged with his grandchildren in ways he never gave to me but just stuffed it down, grateful for the dramatic changes in him.

Shortly after his seventieth birthday, my father developed a knot behind his right knee that turned out to be cancer. He endured radiation and tried chemo for a while, looking sunburned and red as a lobster. For over a year, he battled and gave it his all, comforted by the love of my mother, the support of friends, and the community at their church. I flew back and forth between Denver and Nashville as often as I could. Daddy was usually too tired to talk about more than football or the weather. On good days, he would joke and try to eat solid food instead of just downing his daily can of Ensure.

During my visits we had a couple of serious talks, bouncing from topic to topic—my marriage and career, my kids, his memories of my childhood, his days as a dirt track race car driver, his relationship with my mother—but all pulled together into orbit by the inevitable gravity of his passing. He never outright asked me to forgive him for some of the crazy hard times when I was growing up, but he did say he was sorry he didn't stop drinking sooner and that he regretted missing out on so much time with me as a kid.

When my father died two weeks after my latest visit, I thought I was prepared. He and I were in a good place, more connected than we'd ever been. The night before he passed, I talked to him on the phone. Dotti had taken the kids to see their Papa one last time, and he lay basking in their love. While my girls served as nurses, my father had my two-year-old son up in bed with him, feeding him potato chips.

The next day when I got the news and flew home, I missed him. I grieved the man he had become, the loving, sober, devoted follower of Jesus, as well as the father I never knew when I was growing up. I was unaware of what I was about to discover at his funeral, a secret requiring a new level of forgiveness.

The Pain of Loving You

Ten minutes before my father's funeral service began, my father's brother, my uncle Frankie Dee (named after President Franklin Delano Roosevelt) pulled me aside and said, "I have someone I want you to meet." I thought nothing of it because all day I'd been meeting and greeting lots of distant kin and childhood friends of my father's. My uncle led me to a group of people talking quietly in the receiving room next to the chapel, and touched the shoulder of a man in a gray suit there, who then turned to face us.

"Dudley," my uncle said as I took the stranger's hand to shake. "I'd like you to meet your brother . . . who is also named *Dudley*." Frankie Dee sounded particularly pleased with himself for making the introduction, as if he just knew we would enjoy meeting one another.

Unable to speak, I nodded and couldn't decide how to wrap my mind around what I had just been told. I wasn't sure what piece of information surprised me more, that I had a brother I'd never met nor heard about, or that we shared the same name, which was also our father's.

I studied the man's appearance as I continued to shake his hand. Clearly older than me by maybe five or six years and shorter by a good four or five inches. Familiar blue-gray eyes set beneath a furrowed forehead, a clean-shaven face and soft jawline, and dark hair slicked back. This man did indeed look like my father, and I didn't doubt for a second the truth of what I had just been told. Unbelievable, nonetheless.

I don't remember much about what happened next. I vaguely recall a second introduction to my new brother's mother, a woman my father dated in between his two

Practice More Than You Preach

marriages. Apparently, when confronted with the news of her pregnancy over forty years prior, my father had denied responsibility and refused to reconcile with her. She had the child, a son whom she named after my father, either out of spite or a last-ditch appeal to his conscience, or both. The other Dudley told me that after adulthood he had tried reaching out to my father a couple times in hopes of having some kind of relationship. He said my father refused and told him to leave him alone.

It was all too much.

I'm not sure whether my brain short-circuited or my heart shattered first, but either way, it was all too much. I felt like laughing in that hysterical, barking-dog kind of way that you see in cartoons and sitcoms when someone goes crazy. With the organ music starting, I glanced up at the clock and saw it strike two; most everyone was seated and the service was about to start. I excused myself to the men's room and splashed cold water on my face. Looking in the mirror, I searched for traces of the same face I had just seen, as well as the one with eyes closed lying in the open casket.

Growing up, I never knew what I'd find when I came home from school. No matter what I expected, my father always managed to surprise me. His death was no different. One last punch in the gut.

It's now been over ten years since my father died and I learned of an older half-brother who shares our father's name with me (fortunately, we have different middle names). Over time, I came to forgive my father and to realize that my pain and disappointment had little to nothing to do with discovering his previous relationship and the son it produced. It had almost everything to do with his secret shame, the weight he must have felt all those years, and his refusal to accept responsibility for this other son. In addition to the pain he caused in others' lives, I fear my daddy wasn't able to forgive himself.

As my own children are now entering adulthood, I know they're coming to terms with seeing their parents differently. I don't have any bombshell disclosures to drop on them, but I know I still need their forgiveness nevertheless. My wife and I have loved them the best we can but remain aware of our mistakes and shortcomings. We're grateful for the love we all share despite the times when we don't get along or don't particularly like each other.

We've tried to teach our kids that forgiveness, both of ourselves and others, is an essential part of being human—and one we can't complete on our own. It's further reason for practicing faith and relying on God's mercy. I'm challenged daily to "Get rid of all bitterness, rage and anger, brawling and slander, along with every form of malice. Be kind and compassionate to one another, forgiving each other, just as in Christ God forgave you" (Ephesians 4:31–32). But the truth is, I can only forgive anyone if I'm mindful of how much I'm forgiven.

of Tennessee class," April 14, 2017, *Knox News*, https://www.knoxnews.com/story/news/education/2017/04/14/dolly-parton-tweets-approval-university-tennessee-class/100460294/.
12. Leigh H. Edwards, *Dolly Parton, Gender, and Country Music* (Bloomington, IN: Indiana Univ. Press, 2018) at http://www.iupress.indiana.edu/product_info.php?products_id=808973.
13. Parton, *My Life and Other Unfinished Business*, 89.
14. Ibid., 27–28.
15. Ibid., 210.
16. Nash, *Dolly*, 165.

Chapter 10: Read into the Future

1. "The Buddy Program," Last updated August 23, 2015, *Dolly*, https://dollyparton.com/imagination_library/buddy-program/1591.
2. https://imaginationlibrary.com/.
3. www.imaginationlibrary.com/letter-from-Dolly/, accessed January 6, 2018.
4. Amy Maclin, "Life Lessons from Dolly Parton on Beauty, Marriage and Happiness," O, *The Oprah Magazine* (June 2016) at http://www.oprah.com/inspiration/dolly-parton-on-marriage-and-happiness.

Notes

3. Ibid., 234–235.
4. Cliff Jahr, "How I Came Close to Suicide," *Ladies' Home Journal* (June 1986): 78–82.
5. Parton, *My Life and Other Unfinished Business*, 236.
6. Parton, *Dream More*, 45.

Chapter 9: Laugh First to Make Love Last

1. Parton, *My Life and Other Unfinished Business*, 190–191.
2. Dolly Parton, Press Conference, National Press Club, Washington, D.C., March 23, 2000.
3. David Reed, "Dolly Interview," *Lexington Herald-Leader* (March 9, 1979) in *Dolly on Dolly: Interviews and Encounters with Dolly Parton*, Randy L. Schmidt, ed. (Chicago: Chicago Review Press, 2017), 154.
4. Jonathan Zilberg, "Yes, It's True: Zimbabweans Love Dolly Parton," *The Journal of Popular Culture* 29, no. 1 (Summer 1995): 111–125.
5. "Glastonbury performance draws over 180,000," Last updated August 23, 2015, *Dolly*, https://dollyparton.com/life-and-career/glastonbury-performance/5744.
6. Parton, *Dream More*, 107.
7. Ibid., 108.
8. Ibid., 104.
9. "12 Best Quips from Dolly's Return to the Ryman," August 3, 2015, *The Bluegrass Situation*, https://thebluegrasssituation.com/read/12-best-quips-from-dollys-return-to-the-ryman.
10. Jacey Fortin, "Dolly Parton College Course Combines Music, History and Appalachia Pride," April 20, 2017, *The New York Times*, https://www.nytimes.com/2017/04/20/us/dolly-parton-college-course.html.
11. Rachel Ohm, "Dolly Parton tweets approval of University

10. Ibid.
11. Parton, *My Life and Other Unfinished Business*, 182.
12. Ibid.
13. Ibid., 173.
14. Gerri Hirshey, "Good Golly, Miss Dolly," *Ladies' Home Journal* (March 2008), 48–50.

Chapter 6: Baby Steps toward a Leap of Faith

1. Tim Hollis and Mitzi Soward, *Lost Attractions of Sevier County* (Charleston, SC: Arcadia Publishing, 2011), 49–54.
2. Scot Haller, "Dolly Parton: Come On Down to Dollywood," *People* 25, no. 18 (May 5, 1986): http://people.com/archive/cover-story-dolly-parton-come-on-down-to-dollywood-vol-25-no-18/.
3. Parton, *Dream More*, 53.

Chapter 7: Let Your Roots Keep You Grounded

1. Kim Severson, "Dollywood," August 22, 2014, *New York Times*, www.nytimes.com/2014/08/24/travel/dollywood-a-little-bit-country-a-little-bit-gay.html.
2. Parton, *My Life and Other Unfinished Business*, 165.
3. Parton, *Dream More*, 14.
4. Meagan Murphy, "Dolly Parton Says Giving Back Has Nothing To Do with Being Rich," June 13, 2011, *Fox News Entertainment*, http://www.foxnews.com/entertainment/2011/06/13/for-dolly-parton-giving-back-has-nothing-to-do-with-being-rich.html.
5. Parton, *My Life and Other Unfinished Business*, 219.

Chapter 8: Shine through the Shadows

1. Ibid., 231.
2. Ibid., 234.

Notes

5. Parton, *Dream More*, 71.
6. Aman, "So This Is Why We Never See Dolly Parton's Husband."
7. Parton, *My Life and Other Unfinished Business*, 197.
8. Ibid., 202.
9. "Honoring Don Warden: 'Mr. Everything,'" Last updated March 13, 2017, *Dolly*, https://dollyparton.com/life-and-career/honoring-don-warden/13752.
10. Parton, *Dream More*, 75.

Chapter 5: Practice More Than You Preach

1. Nash, *Dolly*, 24.
2. Ibid., 25.
3. Parton, *Dream More*, 62.
4. Joseph Neese, "15 quotes from Dolly Parton that teach us everything about life," January 19, 2016, MSNBC, http://www.msnbc.com/msnbc/15-quotes-dolly-parton-teach-us-everything-about-life.
5. https://www.nps.gov/grsm/learn/nature/geology.htm#10/35.6238/-83.5757.
6. "Sevierville 'Dolly Days' Honor Dolly," Last updated August 23, 2015, *Dolly*, https://dollyparton.com/life-and-career/sevierville-dolly-days/5171.
7. Jack Hurst, "Miss Dolly Parton: Blonde Bombshell of Great Smokies," *The Tennessean* (September 27, 1970), 2.
8. Diane Swanbrow, "Empathy: College students don't have as much as they used to," May 27, 2010, *Michigan News*, http://ns.umich.edu/new/releases/7724-empathy-college-students-don-t-have-as-much-as-they-used-to.
9. Beverly Keel, "Dolly Parton's Biggest Part Is Her … Heart," December 4, 2015, *Parade*, https://parade.com/440799/beverlykeel/give-like-dolly-does/2/.

5. https://dollyparton.com/life-and-career/awards_milestones/grand-ole-opry-performance-1959/5142.
6. Ibid.
7. Jack Hurst, *Chicago Tribune* (January 31, 1976) in *Dolly on Dolly: Interviews and Encounters with Dolly Parton*, Randy L. Schmidt, ed. (Chicago: Chicago Review, 2017), 2.
8. Dolly Parton, *Dream More: Celebrate the Dreamer in You* (New York: Riverhead/Penguin, 2012), 15.

Chapter 3: Know When to Stretch Your Wings

1. Parton, *My Life and Other Unfinished Business*, 182.
2. Ibid., 186.
3. Chet Flippo, "Interview: Dolly Parton," *Rolling Stone* (August 25, 1977), (https://www.rollingstone.com/music/features/dolly-parton-19770825).
4. Ibid.
5. Ibid.
6. Ibid.
7. Ibid.

Chapter 4: Love like a Butterfly While Busy as a Bee

1. Parton, *My Life and Other Unfinished Business*, 141.
2. Melanie Aman, "So This Is Why We Never See Dolly Parton's Husband," Last updated August 29, 2017, *Woman's World*, http://www.womansworld.com/posts/dolly-parton-husband-carl-dean-133672.
3. Dolly Parton, *My Life and Other Unfinished Business*, 141.
4. "Exhibit Marks 30th Anniversary of Dolly Parton Statue in Sevierville," March 15, 2017, *Sevier News Messenger*, http://www.seviernewsmessenger.com/2017/03/15/30th-anniversary-dolly-parton-statue/.

Notes

Chapter 1: Dream Your Way Forward

1. Alanna Nash, *Dolly* (Los Angeles: Reed Books/A *Country Music Magazine* Book, 1978), 12.
2. Cliff Jahr, "How I Came Close to Suicide," *Ladies' Home Journal* (June 1986): 78–82.
3. Dolly Parton, *My Life and Other Unfinished Business* (New York: HarperCollins, 1994), 83.
4. Ibid., 69–70.
5. Ibid., 77.
6. Ibid., 78.
7. Ibid., 3.
8. Ibid., 39.
9. Nash, *Dolly*, 342.

Chapter 2: You Need Wings to Fly

1. Ajay Kalra, "Cas Walker," *The Encyclopedia of Appalachia* (Knoxville, TN: University of Tennessee Press, 2006), 544–545.
2. Parton, *My Life and Other Unfinished Business*, 99.
3. https://twitter.com/dollyparton/status/567789578342645760?lang=en.
4. Nash, *Dolly*, 51.

The Faith of Dolly Parton

Dotti, wow, if I could, I would ask Dolly to write a song just for you to express my deepest gratitude. It would be a love song, of course, and let you know that if I had it all to do over again, you are the only one for me. Thanks for putting up with me and my crazy writer's way of life. Thanks for loving Dolly as much as I do. I love you, honey. Our adventure continues!

Acknowledgments

Jim Arnold, Joe Gipson, Bob Gipson, Janna Thacher Findley, Sherrie Cleek Kaiser, and the gang—thank you for welcoming me back so warmly. More than ever, I'm grateful for friendships that endure over the years.

Barry and Rhonda Tawwater remind me how much family means and how good it feels to come home to Tennessee. Thank you for welcoming my family and me in so many ways. I'm so grateful to my mother, Norma Delffs, for all her prayers, encouragement, homecookin', and loving support over the years. Thank you, Mama, for my love of books and reading and for roots that run deep.

Back in Michigan, a big shout-out to my guys, Justin Reed, Mark Petrowski, and Kevin Kelling. I couldn't ask for better friends and prayer partners in crime. Now I just have to get you all to move to Tennessee!

Ron Winfree, you are family to me—thank you. Whether you're serving as accountant, counselor, home repair expert, tour guide, mentor, or friend, I don't know what I'd do without you. I appreciate your support and encouragement through the writing process more than you can know.

My children—Mary Elise, Annie, and Jacob—I love you so much and continue to marvel as you spread your wings and leave the nest. I'm so proud of you as you make your way and find your place in the world. You have each encouraged me in special ways during the writing of this book. You remind me why I do what I do and how blessed I am to have you all in my life.

The Faith of Dolly Parton

I appreciate the help of Kim Tanner, Bridgette Brooks, Keith Finnegan, and the many other team members on board.

In addition to sharing my love for Dolly, my editor, Carolyn McCready, provided so much assurance, encouragement, and expertise. I'm so grateful for her guidance each step of the way. Carolyn, you're the best.

Ami McConnell, another Tennessean and my sister in the order of the Dolly Mama, I can't thank you enough for all you poured into making my writing stronger and clearer. Your heart for the project came through even as your keen edits and thoughtful insight made me a better writer. Thank you, Ami!

I'm so blessed to have a publisher who is also my good friend. David Morris, this book would not exist without your call that summer afternoon and your immediate enthusiasm for my somewhat unorthodox idea. You not only encouraged me at crucial points in the writing, you urged me to embrace the surprising direction that it took. I appreciate all you've done, both personally and professionally, to bring this book to life.

A host of folks in Tennessee helped me and contributed to the writing of this book. In the Volunteer State, I'm grateful to Sydney Ford, my sister-in-law, for her memories of Cas Walker; to Lucy Hill for her kindness and expertise in helping my family make the move; to Allen Reddick for his friendship and the use of his beautiful, historic home in Sewanee on Morgan's Steep.

To old friends and classmates—Steve and Kim Arnold,

Acknowledgments

I'm so grateful to Dolly Parton for the way she has lived out her faith her whole life. Thank you, Dolly, for the many ways you inspire me, along with so many others, to be true to myself and faithful to God. Thank you for your music, your generosity, your love. Following your frequent example, I thank God for having more blessings in my life than I deserve, including the joy of writing this book.

Dolly is also quick to give credit where credit is due. She knows that any creative endeavor requires a collaborative spirit and a ton of hard work. During the writing process, I was reminded once again of how much I rely on the support, encouragement, and shared vision of so many friends and family, as well as the other writers whose work informed my research. I have tried to credit you all accurately and represent your context with integrity. Any mistakes are mine, not yours.

I'm thankful for my friends at Zondervan, both old and new, who immediately caught my vision for this book.

The Faith of Dolly Parton

- 🦋 Why do you think this song is your favorite? How does it make you feel? What memories and associations does it evoke in you?
- 🦋 What does the song you selected say about Dolly and how you view her? Why? What does it say about you and your own faith?

Dear God,

I'm grateful for Dolly and the way she has lived out her faith throughout her career. Regardless of how different my life may be compared to hers, I want to be the same kind of positive influence on those around me. Thank you for loving me and for the many gifts and blessings in my life. Help me to grow closer to you, trusting you more and more each day. Like Dolly, let me leave a legacy that will bless others for generations to come.

Amen.

Read into the Future

Divine Dose of Dolly

Give, and it will be given to you. Good measure, pressed down, shaken together, running over, will be put into your lap. For with the measure you use it will be measured back to you.
LUKE 6:38, ESV

- What has been your favorite part of this book? Why? What have you learned about Dolly's life that you didn't already know? Did this change the way you view her? Why or why not?
- How has learning more about Dolly's faith inspired you in your own faith? What ultimately will you remember about what you've read here?

Listen to your favorite Dolly Parton song, the one that you absolutely love the most. As you listen, try to remember the first time you heard it, what you were doing, and how you felt after listening to it.

a song I know, whether I'm alone in my truck or in the grocery store. I'm going to wear what I want to wear. I may even get another tattoo!"

We all laughed again, but I was serious. Dolly inspires me because she encourages me to be my best self, to go all in, to keep hoping, even when I've lived more than long enough to feel cynical at times. She reminds me to take both failure and success in stride and not to miss out on loving the special people in my life during the finite time we have together. She doesn't slow down and refuses to quit risking, creating, and giving.

Dolly has aged as gracefully as anyone I've ever seen, not just in maintaining her famous figure, beautiful face, and blonde wigs. Her luminous spirit, big heart, and fertile imagination remain as lively and dynamic as when she was a girl chasing butterflies in the hollers of East Tennessee. She's never slowed down and has repeatedly said she will never retire. "I hope to fall over dead onstage right in the middle of a song," Dolly has said. "I'd be making music even if I had to sell records out of the back of my car."[4]

I will always love Dolly because she helps me to reconsider my faith and the role it plays in my life. She reminds me, along with countless others, to keep going, to work at being happy, to never give up hope, to pursue what I love, and to expect God's presence and blessing in the midst of it all. Whatever else you may take away from this book and our time together, I hope you've been encouraged to see Dolly's faith—as well as your own—in new ways.

Read into the Future

I suspect many of us felt this way as children, that we were special, different from others by the sheer expression of our personality and creativity. But as we grow up and become socialized, learning the rules of how to get along with others—especially with our families—maybe we sacrifice our uniqueness. We go with the flow and do what it takes to be accepted, to fit in, to get the approval of others. Dolly's example, however, reminds us of the joy of being uniquely who we are and trusting God with the rest.

Studying Dolly's life so intensively and writing this book has certainly had a positive impact on me. As I'm writing this, only a handful of days remain in this year. With all three of our adult children home for the holidays, my family enjoyed one last meal together before everyone went their separate ways to Colorado, Michigan, and Tennessee. At dinner someone asked if anyone was making resolutions for the new year or setting new goals for themselves. We each went around the table, and when it was my turn, I said, "I'm going to be as weird as I want to be!"

My family and I laughed together, and then I explained what I meant. "I'm over fifty years old now and I'm tired of trying to please everybody or act like I'm an average, middle-aged adult. After reading so much about Dolly's life and writing my book, I feel more like a kid than ever before. I'm going to get up and dance at the next wedding reception I attend. I'm going to sing along when I hear

The Faith of Dolly Parton

backlash from people who know what they're really like? You can see the risks, at least from a business perspective.

I'm grateful there are exceptions, however, because Dolly has proven herself and her faith are real. Again, she's no saint and, in fact, seems to enjoy making mischief and embarrassing others with a sexy joke or flirtatious comment. She slips into salty language on occasion, unafraid to cuss a little, usually to make a point or land a punch line. But the jokes, the flirting, the language only remind us she's honest. As the lady I overheard in line at Dollywood said, "I just love Dolly 'cause she's still like me." She's not perfect, never claimed to be, and gives us all permission to be human.

Dolly has been in the public eye for over six decades now. That little blonde pixie singing with all her heart in front of a live audience for Cas Walker's radio show has reached the highest heights of celebrity stardom and not only sustained her fame but also demonstrated what it looks like to live out her faith in the global fishbowl of spotlights, sound bites, and social media. She's the real deal.

Like any true artist, Dolly stirs something in us not only through her art, her music and songwriting, performing and storytelling, but in the way she lives her life. Always striving for more, to be the best Dolly she can be, she inspires you and me to believe in ourselves again, to hope that maybe there's something special about us after all.

American dream achieved, a rags-to-riches story fueled by sheer talent, gritty determination, hard work, and an unwavering ability to be true to herself and her values. She inspires us not only for her success but for how she handles her success and what she does with it. Over the past decades, many entertainers have attained wealth and fame, but arguably few have handled it with the grace, gratitude, and gumption of Dolly.

We Will Always Love You, Dolly

When I worked in Christian publishing, we were usually leery of celebrity books. My bosses had been around long enough to know that so-called celebrities would often come and go according to popular preference and overnight trends, which seems truer than ever with social media and online viral sensations. By the time a book came out, public taste would have changed and the celebrity might be a has-been, a relic like last year's one-hit wonder or that actor whose name you can't remember.

Even when the celebrity had staying power, books about them and their lives seemed risky—especially in our faith-focused markets. What if you had a book about a big star's faith launching just as someone came forward to reveal scandalous behavior or a secret addiction? What if the person wasn't so nice and faith-full below the surface of their public persona and a new book caused a fierce

The Faith of Dolly Parton

Simply put, Dolly Parton is now an icon, a word that gets used more these days, even as the people truly worthy of it become fewer. Interestingly enough, *icon* is also one of those words that's evolved to encompass both religious and secular meanings. Deriving from the Greek *eikon*, the word literally means image or likeness. In the early nineteenth century, however, the word was used to name the small religious artifacts turning up in homes, churches, and other places of worship.

During this time, the early 1800s, Christians from Eastern churches began emigrating to Western Europe and the United States, bringing along squares of wood hand-painted with the likeness of Jesus, Mary, and various saints from home. Around for hundreds of years, these works were often smaller, homemade versions of the sacred artwork enshrined in their churches.

They called these icons and used them to remind them of their home, their faith, and their spiritual roots. Which makes the term icon all the more fitting for Dolly Parton. She'll be the first one to tell you she's no saint, but talk with her long enough, and you'll also realize just how important her Christian faith is to her. Not because she uses religious jargon heard in churches or tries to preach at you. Just the opposite—Dolly shares her faith in honest responses to hard questions, through her humility and sense of humor, but more important, by what she does with her wealth and celebrity.

Dolly Parton inspires us because she represents the

style of the old Hatch Show Print posters made famous by the Grand Ole Opry that simply says, "What would Dolly do?"

Close to My Heart

My desire to move back to Tennessee coincided with the opportunity to write a book close to my heart, a hope-filled little book about the faith of Dolly Parton.

This coincidence caused me to see just how much I admire and appreciate Dolly as an ongoing presence throughout my life, always reminding me of home, of my dreams, and of the faith that sustains my journey. Like her millions of fans around the world, I love Dolly for many reasons, which I've shared with you throughout these pages.

With her larger-than-life personality, self-deprecating one-liners, signature glamour, enormous talent, and honest faith, Dolly has established herself as a multifaceted diamond in a rhinestone world, continually sparkling, shining, and surprising her many fans, both old and new. She can joke about her anatomy one minute, play a new song she's just written the next, reveal the latest addition to her Dollywood theme park, or gush about her Imagination Library giving away over one hundred million books to children around the world. And tying all these threads together is her plainspoken, true-to-her-roots faith in God.

What Would Dolly Do?

The journey of writing this book has not been what I expected. I thought it would just be a good excuse to dive deeper into my love for Dolly, point out some things about her life and faith you might not have noticed or thought about, and encourage you to keep going and keep believing. I pray it's been all that and more for you.

For me, it's been a way to think about various milestones in my life and to look ahead to others I dream about. I've wept many times as I've tried to share with you both the hard times and high points of my life. While I've been known to shed a tear or two, I was not prepared for the fountain dribbling down my cheeks and beard. I've also laughed on a daily basis more than I can ever remember, because every day I would run across a new story from Dolly's life, a quote I hadn't heard before, or an interview I hadn't read. I've had the pleasure of listening to hours and hours of the songs she's written and recorded, some I hadn't thought of in years and others that were new to me entirely.

Early on, I discovered that I couldn't just cut and paste some facts from Dolly's life and retell some stories. If I was going to make this worthwhile, I was going to have to write from my heart, share some of my story, and reveal part of my soul. I was going to have to do what Dolly does and does so well. No wonder my wife gave me one of my favorite Christmas presents ever this year, a print in the

Read into the Future

The greatest praise, at least for its founder, likely comes from the man who inspired her to launch the program. Dolly shares, "Before he passed away, my Daddy told me the Imagination Library was probably the most important thing I had ever done. I can't tell you how much that meant to me because I created the Imagination Library as a tribute to my Daddy. He was the smartest man I have ever known but I know in my heart his inability to read probably kept him from fulfilling all of his dreams. Inspiring kids to love to read became my mission."[3]

I agree with Mr. Parton. The thing for which Dolly Parton will be most remembered may have nothing to do with her iconic appearance, her down-home sense of humor, or even her amazing body of award-winning hit songs. In fact, Dolly has shared that many kids know her only as "the book lady," unaware of her fame and celebrity from all her other creative endeavors. In my humble opinion, Dolly's Imagination Library will have the greatest impact on the most lives. In many ways it already has.

It seems fitting that on the program's website (www.imaginationlibrary.com) is a picture of Dolly reading *The Little Engine That Could* by Watty Piper, a classic tale of perseverance for generations of children. Fitting because Dolly has not only proven that she could, but she has made a huge difference—a positive legacy for generations to come. And she ain't through yet!

following year, and Australia a few years later. As I write this, the Imagination Library is preparing to celebrate giving away its *one hundred millionth* book. Dolly says, "You can never get enough books into the hands of enough children."[2]

Since it began over two decades ago, the book-gifting nonprofit program has won numerous awards, been lauded by dozens of leaders, and remains a worthy cause championed by thousands of contributors, supporters, and volunteers. The Imagination Library has earned The Good Housekeeping Seal of Approval, the Best Practices Award from the Library of Congress, and recognition validating the impact it is making from Reading Psychology.

Dolly with some participants of her Imagination Library, 2007.

Read into the Future

Robert Lee Parton, as well as rescue others from illiteracy. In 1995, she launched Dolly Parton's Imagination Library. The concept is simple: give books to children before they get to school. This idea wasn't simply supported by her own experience but by research showing that children from working class, lower income homes usually don't learn to read prior to first grade.

On the other hand, a majority of children from middle class families often begin reading before school, having been read to throughout childhood. This crucial difference often burdens some children with an educational handicap out of the gate. These students feel dumb, become self-conscious, and don't like school because of the way it makes them feel less than their peers.

Regardless of a family's income level, Dolly's Imagination Library mails age-appropriate books to children, free of charge, from birth until they turn six, which is the age many begin school. The books are first-rate, high quality, not discarded or secondhand copies. Initially, the program only distributed books to children living in Dolly's home of Sevier County, Tennessee. It caught on so quickly, however, that within a few short years, the entire state participated, with public and government support. From the Volunteer State, the program spread throughout the country, and by 2003, the Imagination Library had mailed out its one millionth book.

And it didn't stop there. In 2006, the program began serving Canada, followed by the United Kingdom the

The Faith of Dolly Parton

There was also our local library, of course, with the wonderful Mrs. Lunsford who would set aside books especially for me, ones she knew would make me laugh or keep me in suspense. As I approached adolescence, I discovered new friends through the library—from Charlotte and Wilbur on to Bilbo and Frodo and then Sam Spade and Hercule Poirot. I also checked out a few titles I knew my parents probably wouldn't have let me read, mostly by authors like Stephen King, Michael Crichton, and Robin Cook. Then on to classics like *Call of the Wild*, *Moby-Dick*, *The Great Gatsby*, and *To Kill a Mockingbird*.

Yeah, no wonder I'm a book geek, right?

Thank goodness I'm not the only one who believes books have the power to change our lives. Dolly has often talked about the way she loved to read as a child but didn't have much reading material other than the Bible, a few catalogs, and old newspapers used to insulate the cracks in their drafty mountain cabin. She also witnessed firsthand the painful limitations of illiteracy, seeing her daddy ask others to read letters or newspapers to him. Dolly recalls that when it was time to bring home her report card from school to get a parent's signature, she confessed to her father that she wasn't worried about making bad grades because she knew she could forge his signature. He laughed and said, "Of course you can! What's so hard about making an X?"

The laughter in that memory is bittersweet, though, and Dolly found an amazing way to honor her father, up with a buddy and helped those who needed a buddy find one. She then promised $500 to each of them if both they *and* their buddy graduated—they both had to graduate in order to receive the cash!

Dolly's plan worked and proved to be a huge success, cutting the drop-out rate from 35 percent to about 6 percent.[1] It also brought ongoing public attention and community support for students to complete their high school education, not only in Sevier County but across the state and throughout the nation. The program continues to this day, often supplemented by special scholarships and fund-raisers.

Books Make a Difference

Growing up, I loved books almost as much as I loved my granny's homemade rice pudding. They were my friends, my consolers, my educators, my informers, my inspiration, my entertainment, and my aspiration. I was fortunate because books were surprisingly plentiful in our house, thanks to my mother. While some kids beg for a candy bar or small toy every time they go to the store, I found books irresistible. All I had to do was ask, and almost always my mom found a way. Whether ordering from the monthly Scholastic Book Club at school, waiting for the latest Batman comic book, or buying my beloved Hardy Boys mysteries at the nearest B. Dalton bookstore, I was always reading. Thanks, Mama.

those generations following behind her. You see evidence of her dedication to improve the lives of others with the establishment of The Dollywood Foundation in 1988 (www.dollywoodfoundation.org), in particular its two pet projects, the Buddy Program and the Imagination Library.

As I shared, earlier in her career Dolly performed a benefit concert and recorded a live album in Sevierville at her old high school. She donated the proceeds to establish a scholarship fund for students there and promised to keep it funded, which she has faithfully done. But as she began interacting with administrators and educators, she learned there was a serious problem: over a third of students dropped out before graduating, much higher than the averages of most schools in most states.

Digging into it deeper, Dolly learned the problem started much earlier. Around the time students transitioned from elementary to middle school, around seventh and eighth grade, many students begin making decisions, cementing study habits, and choosing courses that determined their trajectory. If they struggled and had no vision for their futures, many figured why not drop out of school and get a job.

So Dolly decided to provide a little incentive. In 1991, she invited all the seventh and eighth graders in Sevier County to a special assembly at Dollywood. There she revealed her newly formed Buddy Program, a planned incentive to encourage each and every one of them to finish their high school education. Dolly had students pair

CHAPTER 10

Read into the Future

> *My desire to pursue my dreams has always been greater than my fear of not accomplishing them.*
> DOLLY PARTON

The first few notes of "Jolene" instantly pull at your heart. And just try not to sing along to "Islands in the Stream"—it's nearly impossible. Her songs are legendary. Her image is iconic. But Dolly's ultimate legacy may have nothing to do with music.

One of the most dynamic, exemplary ways she lives out her faith is through her commitment to give back to those following in her footsteps. In addition to brightening the lives of millions of fans with her songs and concerts, and on top of the many wonderful causes she supports with her time, energy, and financial resources, Dolly has consistently demonstrated a soft spot for children and the power of literacy and education in their lives. She has given back not only to her family and her fans but also to

The Faith of Dolly Parton

> *Dear God,*
>
> *Laughter truly is a gift from you! Thank you for my sense of humor and the ability to share it with others. Help me to use my humor to build bridges and never to hurt or demean others. Thank you for all the joy that we experience from our ability to laugh.*
>
> *Amen.*

Divine Dose of Dolly

A cheerful heart is good medicine.
PROVERBS 17:22

- Do you think of yourself as having a good sense of humor? How would you describe it? What kinds of things do you usually find funny or amusing?
- What do you enjoy most about the way Dolly uses humor? What are some of your favorite jokes or one-liners from her repertoire? Do you agree that her sense of humor allows her to build bridges with others? Why or why not?

Listen to Dolly sing "Backwoods Barbie" or "PMS Blues" before answering the following questions.

- What lyrics made you laugh or smile in this song? What struck you funny about it?
- How does this song illustrate Dolly's ability to use humor to convey a deeper message? What message do you think she's relaying through this song? Why?

going around, "What's worse than a giraffe with a sore throat? Dolly Parton with a chest cold!"

Dolly without her sense of humor would not be Dolly. That little-girl giggle, that mischievous grin, the twinkle in her eye—they make it impossible not to share the joke with her. Dolly learned to laugh first to make our love for her last long after the punch line. Her humor reflects a faith that looks for the best in life, and if it doesn't find it, then it finds something else to laugh about.

Either way, the result is joy, a joy that remains contagious.

her place—must have been quite hurtful. No one, not even Dolly Parton, likes being objectified, dehumanized, and dismissed.

Dolly with Miss Piggy

She quickly caught on, however, and it's no accident that her first big hit, "Dumb Blonde," looked the issue square in the eye. Soon she learned to quip that it didn't bother her if others called her a dumb blonde—because she knew she wasn't dumb, and she knew she wasn't blonde!

By being the one to joke first, Dolly displays a keen sense of self-awareness. She refuses to take herself too seriously. On an early appearance on *The Tonight Show* in the eighties, Dolly told Johnny Carson a joke she'd heard

The Faith of Dolly Parton

They know that sharing a laugh together breaks the ice and builds a bridge. Humor can be so effective at disarming others, showing them that you don't take yourself too seriously and that you're just like them in your ability to find something funny. Even when the jokes are familiar, the punch lines corny, and the humor falls flat, most folks at least appreciate the effort. One writer observed of Dolly, "She can lay the lamest, hoariest gag on a sophisticated audience and reap gales of laughter, simply by attaching her own bemused giggle at the end."[16]

Simply put, she's in on the joke.

Dolly knows this secret and uses it exceptionally well. Many of her jokes about herself are the same and have been recycled faithfully depending on the occasion. But her fans don't mind and instead enjoy her familiar sense of humor and that high, little-girl laugh for which she's famous. They also know she's quick on her feet and that her wit is sharp enough to keep up with anyone, from Porter Wagoner to Barbara Walters, Pee-wee Herman to Miss Piggy, from Johnny Carson to Jimmy Fallon.

Dolly loves telling jokes on herself, and many people have speculated that part of her motivation is to pre-empt others' attempts to laugh at her or look down on her. Apparently when she first arrived in Nashville, ambitious yet naïve about the music industry, she wasn't prepared for others to perceive her as a dumb blonde. I'm sure some of those early comments and wisecracks from others— probably mostly men trying to hit on her or keep her in

Punch Line in the Pulpit

Recently I heard about a senior pastor who asked his church's youth pastor to fill in for him while he was out of town. Knowing the younger man's style was much more casual and fly-by-the-seat-of-your-pants than his own thoroughly researched and tightly structured sermons, the senior pastor warned, "You're going to have to up your game, son. You can't just wing it, okay? This is Sunday morning, prime time!"

"Yes, sir," agreed the young pastor, fresh out of Bible college.

The following Sunday evening, the senior pastor returned home from his trip, eager to hear how things had gone that morning.

"How was it?" he asked his wife.

"Not good," she said. "Honestly, it was probably the worst sermon I've ever heard in my life. And I know I'm not the only one who felt this way."

Dreading his conversation with his young associate, on Monday morning the senior pastor asked him, "So, how did it go yesterday? Good sermon?"

"Yes, it was—praise the Lord!" The younger pastor looked at him and smiled. "I got so nervous because of what you said that I ran out of time—so I just used one of your old sermons!"

Pastors and preachers have a long tradition of using humor to connect with their audiences and congregations.

The Faith of Dolly Parton

in Louisville, Kentucky, Dolly usually opened her shows at the time with the classic song "Higher and Higher."

So there she was on stage, embracing the high-energy crowd with her opening number, when Dolly heard a too-familiar voice behind her. She was surprised because Carl usually didn't typically travel with her or attend her concerts, and rarely if ever appeared backstage. Without missing a beat, Dolly glanced behind her and saw her husband beside her two regular back-up singers, just cutting loose (fortunately, Carl has a good voice).

Dolly wasn't about to let it go, thinking, "I just couldn't let him get one on me without some kind of retaliation. What kind of fun-loving wife would I be?"[15] So she finished the song without acknowledging her husband's presence onstage behind her, and while her band prepared for the next number, Dolly casually went to the edge of the stage where a local policeman was stationed as part of security for the show.

Dolly pointed out Carl, by this time wandering backstage, as a suspicious stranger, telling the officer she feared that he might be a stalker. As the show resumed, Dolly took the stage again while the policeman apprehended Carl and prepared to take him in for questioning. Fortunately, Dolly's longtime manager and friend Don Warden passed them, recognized Carl, and informed the officer. Afterward, Carl didn't mention the incident to his famous wife—and never has. Apparently, the two of them refuse to let the other one have the last laugh.

Laugh First to Make Love Last

One of the funniest stories Dolly tells is about how her uncle Dot Watson, married to her mother's sister Estelle, once sent the Parton kids off on a wild pony chase. Visiting his nieces and nephews there at their little farmstead in the mountains, Uncle Dot, likely with a gleam in his eye but without cracking a smile, told the kids they could "grow a pony" if they just planted the right "pony seeds," which—you guessed it—basically meant them going around and collecting dried manure to plant in their garden.

Each visit her uncle would ask how the ponies were growing. When they explained they were still pony-less, he would then explain that they must have over-watered the seeds, or perhaps didn't plant them deep enough, or maybe they didn't have enough seeds. So off the kids would go again, collecting horse turds, as Dolly later called them. By the time the kids were old enough to figure out the truth, they didn't care and enjoyed reminiscing about their gullibility and the fun the adults had at their expense. "Uncle Dot was living proof that the spirit of mischief that naturally crops up in a kid does not necessarily end with adulthood."[14]

Dolly's right about the spirit of mischief not ending with adulthood, because her husband Carl Dean seems to match her prank for prank, perhaps one of the secrets to their over-fifty-year marriage. Dolly has shared how Carl loves to back her up, so he surprised her once and literally did just that. Set to perform at a large outdoor venue at a rodeo

Willadeene's husband, a special show. Apparently, Willadeene had always encouraged her younger sister in her musical aspirations, comparing her to stars such as Brenda Lee. Because Dolly sang so well, Willadeene began asking Dolly to wait near the road to their home and sing for June as he drove up.

Flattered, Dolly loved the attention until one day she was waiting for June and became inspired to do more than welcome him with her voice. Hopping on to an old tree swing, she shucked her drawers and waited until she saw her sister's beau before mooning him from the tree while singing her own revised version of "On Top of Old Smokey."[13]

This was not the only time Dolly would expose herself to get a laugh. In Hollywood filming *9 to 5* and driving around one night with a group of girlfriends, Dolly couldn't resist Judy Ogle's double dare to streak through sexy singer Tom Jones's yard. Without a stitch on, Dolly left her friends in stitches and fortunately didn't get arrested. Dolly has also been known to reveal her most famous assets on select occasions, particularly to shock close friends such as manager Sandy Gallin. Apparently, that urge to reveal herself lingered long after mooning her sister's boyfriend!

Dolly is not the only one in her family with a devious sense of humor. She grew up within the heritage of tall tales, exaggerated stories, and outright lies that country people have always appreciated. She experienced firsthand a legacy of laughter.

girl and the voluptuous sex symbol. Emerging through her lyrics, personal stories, stage presence, and visual imagery, these wildly different gender tropes form a central part of Dolly's media image and portrayal of herself as a star and celebrity."[12]

I suspect Dolly never set out to be a figure scrutinized in the classroom. Based on her quick quips and catchy comebacks, she seems much more intent using her humor to connect to people, reminding them that, despite her appearance, she's really just like them. You'll recall the conversations I overheard at my recent visit to Dollywood.

People relate to Dolly because she embodies both the lows and highs, both where they are as well as where they dream about being someday. In addition to her humility and dedication to maintaining her roots, Dolly's humor is the glue that allows her to unite her disparities. She may look like a dolled up drag queen as she often says, but she's as down-to-earth as the girl next door. She may have it all now, but she started with next to nothing.

Joking about these opposites maintains the paradox. It's not a calculated way to manipulate people. It's just who Dolly is. She's just funny that way!

Legacy of Laughter

Dolly has always had a mischievous streak. She recounts how she once gave older sister Willadeene's boyfriend, a young man called June Blalock, who would become in them. More and more, Dolly's appearance, along with her life, career, songs, and impact are being studied by academics and sociologists. My alma mater, the University of Tennessee, has even started offering a course based on Dolly's life, receiving considerable national publicity.

In the past couple of years, UT's History Department has offered a course called "Dolly's America: From Sevierville to the World." More than just an overview of her life and accomplishments, this honors course views modern Appalachian history through the lens of Dolly's life and relationship with the surrounding area. Dr. Lynn Sacco, the professor teaching the course, has observed, "It's really kind of a nerdy class."[10] In typical Dolly fashion, the famous subject of this course responded by tweeting, "From the girl voted in High School 'least likely to succeed' this sure is a blessing!"[11]

Dolly is also at the center of a new book using her life and career to examine shifts in cultural attitudes about gender. Released by Indiana University Press and written by Dr. Leigh H. Edwards, an associate professor of English at Florida State University, the book *Dolly Parton, Gender, and Country Music* explores many of the complexities and paradoxes of Dolly's famous look and appeal to a wide, diverse fan base. Dr. Edwards writes: "Dolly Parton is instantly recognizable for her iconic style and persona, but how did she create her enduring image? Dolly crafted her exaggerated appearance and stage personality by combining two opposing stereotypes—the innocent mountain

Many Colors movie on NBC. With her pretty clothes and exotic perfume, this lady of the night epitomized the feminine wiles that must have seemed from another world to a mountain tomboy who worked in the fields.

With her typical humor, Dolly has frequently described her look as "a blend of Mother Goose, Cinderella, and the local hooker." Her mama and Grandpa Jake, the preacher in her family, of course did not approve of Dolly's "worldly" look, with likely references to Rahab and Jezebel from the Bible. But Dolly remained determined to experiment with all the feminine accouterments, "ammo" in the battle of the sexes as she's called it, despite their objections.

While she had more than one come-to-Jesus meeting, literally, with her stern, conservative preacher grandpa, Dolly would just put on more lipstick and keep going. "He told me I wasn't going to heaven if I kept it up. I said, 'I want to go to heaven, but do I have to look like hell to get there?'"[9] Even when her brothers teased her about looking like a clown because of her excessive makeup, she was undeterred in her quest to look her gaudy best. Needless to say, her family and perhaps the devil himself are no match for the determination of Dolly Parton.

Serious Consideration

While Dolly usually employs humor in describing her life and looks, others are beginning to find serious significance and explains her narrow waist and tiny feet never grew because things don't grow in the shade. After she dies, she expects folks to recognize her grave at the cemetery by the two mounds rising below the headstone.

With such a flashy, exaggerated style of glamour, Dolly expects people to notice her and her body and would probably be disappointed if they didn't. She said she can often discern a man's motives when talking to her by following his line of vision. When she hosted NBC's *Saturday Night Live* in 1989, Dolly's opening monologue had her playing it straight mostly, thanking the cast and crew for being so welcoming, warm, and professional even as the camera closed in and focused entirely on her chest.

According to Dolly, she's always been drawn to makeup, sexy clothes, flashy jewelry, fancy hairdos, perfume, and fingernail polish. As a little girl she would use natural resources to try and achieve the looks she saw in magazines and catalogues, using wild pokeberries to stain her lips burgundy, flour for face powder, and burnt matchsticks for eye makeup. She even tells of cutting shoulder pads out of her granny's coat to use as a makeshift push-up bra when she was a teenager.

As she grew into her teens and made spending money from her Cas Walker earnings, Dolly could finally buy real cosmetics—lipstick, powder, rouge, mascara, and bleach for her hair. Even then she modeled herself after the town tramp, whom Dolly was later delighted to portray in a cameo appearance in her autobiographical *Christmas of* no, it wasn't our old house that made me feel like I'd gone down to Dogpatch to sit a spell. It was the names of the folks who lived there. My wife and I have since come up with our own country nicknames, as well as ones for our kids, but I can't tell you what they are. You might laugh at them.

Universal Language

Dolly frequently jokes about her looks, and perhaps for good reason. If you mention Dolly's name almost anywhere around the world, I'm guessing most people will probably think of the work of her body before her body of work. Her tiny waist, ample bosom, china-doll face, and mane of platinum-gold hair are recognized from Zimbabwe—where sociologists have studied her influence[4]—to Glastonbury, where she broke records with over 180,000 in attendance at the popular British music festival.[5]

Just as well-known as her striking appearance is her self-deprecating, sometimes bawdy humor about the way she looks. She's famous for lines like, "Plastic surgeons are always making mountains out of molehills,"[6] "Home is where I hang my hair,"[7] and "You'd be surprised how much it costs to make a person look this cheap."[8]

The target of most jokes, her two most famous assets might as well be a couple of bull's-eyes. She laughs about not being able to jog because she'd give herself black eyes

The Faith of Dolly Parton

Old Man Hambone passed away—did you know that? I hadn't heard or I would've gone to his funeral. Then at the farmer's market, you know who I saw? You remember that crippled Miller boy? Well, it was his mama, What's Her Name, you know who I'm talkin' about—she said he's going to have another operation end of this month. And then I stopped to see Big'un and Bootsy was there. They said Lil' Bit's not doing so well. May need to go stay with Breezy or Bean Bag."

When he paused to catch his breath, I noticed my wife was looking at me. Her eyes were big, and I could tell she was searching for words. Mama was smiling, used to my father's monologues and their effect on people. After a few seconds, my wife leaned in to my father and said, *"What did you just say? Are those people you mentioned or pet animals? Bootsy? Lil' Bit? Big'un? Crippled Miller Boy? Who in the world are you talking about?"*

We all burst out laughing, even my dad. We weren't laughing at these people but simply the sheer quantity of so many unique nicknames, especially as he'd listed them off. Finally, Daddy said, "No, they're all real people, not dogs or horses or cows or nothin.' That's not their real names, of course, but I don't know if anybody can remember their real names anymore—it's just what everybody calls 'em."

My mother proceeded to go through the list again and try to come up with the given names of the individuals my father had referenced. We were amazed. I realized then, took me awhile to learn how to grow beyond Tennessee while remaining rooted there. One particular incident helped me along the way.

Not long after my wife and I married, we went to visit my parents. They truly loved Dotti like a daughter, and felt comfortable around her, even though she was a "city girl" from a "well-to-do" family in Knoxville. In fact, the first time my parents met Dotti's parents, right after we got engaged, my father went through my entire dating history from middle school until then, naming each girlfriend, her flaws, and why he didn't like her. All leading up to how much he thought of Dotti and why she was perfect for me. I would've been mortified but fortunately had just had my wisdom teeth removed the day before and only heard the happy sounds of Percodan.

At the time of our visit, my parents still lived in the old farmhouse where I'd grown up. While it had all the modern conveniences, I still felt a little self-conscious bringing my wife there. It just seemed, well, more country than I remembered it being. But that trip I realized it wasn't the house that gave it a downhome vibe—it was something I couldn't quite put my finger on.

Dotti, my mama, and I were sitting around talking late one afternoon when we heard my father's pickup roar into the driveway. Joining us, he quickly began telling us where all he'd been and who he saw, which went something like this: "Well, I stopped at the co-op and ran into Buster—he said to tell you hi—and he told me that who can tell you about going to a funeral, the grocery store, or the beauty parlor and have you laughing until you cry. She comes from a long line of Southern storytellers and raconteurs, people with a gift for knowing exactly when and how to exaggerate the truth just enough to make a good story great or a mundane visit to the doctor as funny as a stand-up monologue.

Dolly knows a good sense of humor helps you keep perspective and draws others to you. Laughing instead of crying helps you keep your chin up instead of your head down. Her upbeat personality and love of fun might be dismissed by some as showbiz hype, but I think it's apparent, like almost everything else with Dolly, how much she genuinely loves to laugh. And she never minds if it's at her own expense.

"I make up a lot of Dolly Parton jokes," Dolly said. "Why not? Somebody's got to start them. There are a lot of them I didn't make up that I'd rather somebody hadn't, but I can always joke about myself and the way I look. I think when you get to where you can't joke about yourself, you're in serious trouble."[3]

Name of the Game

Like Dolly, I'm proof that you can take me out of the country but you can't ever take all the country out of me. But it took me awhile to accept this. I wasn't ever ashamed of my upbringing and where I was from, but it

Learn to Laugh

Dolly's sense of humor seems to come naturally. Within her big family, she learned early on the value of laughing instead of crying. When her siblings teased her—or she teased them—she discovered the joy of shared laughter. She took this gift with her and learned that the language of laughter is contagious and universal. Laughter allows you to connect with people, helps them see your personality, and reveals how clever—and humble—you are.

Sometimes you have to laugh so you won't cry. She learned to find humor in just about everything growing up because they had so little. Perhaps this explains why she enjoys telling funny stories about her childhood. One of my favorites focuses on the cramped living conditions and lack of privacy in her overcrowded household. She explains, "Back there in the hills, my folks loved each other, and they loved us. But people say, 'How in the world, living in a small house like that with twelve kids, did you have any privacy?' I say, 'Well, we had a wash pan, and we washed down as far as possible, and then we washed up as far as possible, and when everybody cleared the room, we washed possible."[2]

Humor is just as central to who Dolly is as the Smoky Mountains, country music, and her faith in God. It's not just something she's cultivated as an entertainer—it's simply part of who she is. As my daddy used to say about people, "She a real character!" Dolly is one of those people high tea, and fine dining. Then one night Bob wanted to take her to the opera. Dolly agreed but worried a little. There they were in a beautiful world-class opera house in one of the most historic, cultured cities. Men and women in their tuxedos and couture evening gowns looking like royalty. And Dolly in her tight, spangled dress and big hair.

Despite feeling slightly self-conscious, Dolly took her seat beside Bob and waited for the curtain to go up. When it did, the leading characters in the opera took center stage and began singing in that emotionally charged, intensely dramatic style unique to opera. Their exquisitely trained voices hit each note and enunciated each syllable perfectly.

And Dolly got tickled.

The entire scene just struck her funny. Like those times in church or in school when you can't keep from laughing, Dolly started giggling and tried to stifle it but couldn't. Bob wondered what was going on, as others seated near them cast disapproving glances their way.

Unable to control the laughter bubbling inside her, Dolly decided she better make a run for the bathroom. She barely made her way down the aisle before reaching the ladies' room and collapsing with laughter until tears streamed down her face. She later wrote, "Every time I think of that story, it makes me laugh. I never said I was cultured. . . . if you feel like having a good time, laugh, have it at any cost. Don't ever miss a chance to have fun. Life's too serious most of the time. Just find the humor and laugh, and laugh at yourself, mostly."[1]

CHAPTER 9

Laugh First to Make Love Last

Although I look like a drag queen's Christmas tree on the outside, I am at heart a simple country woman.
DOLLY PARTON

Dolly once brought the Grand Ole Opry to a brand new opera. She was visiting London with a friend from the music industry, Bob Hunka, whom she had met while working with Linda Ronstadt and Emmylou Harris on their *Trio* album. A talented producer, Bob was also a world-class chef, wine connoisseur, art historian, and opera fan. He and Dolly, although about as different as caviar and cornbread, really hit it off and enjoyed traveling together when they could, taking in the famous sights and cultural opportunities wherever they visited.

On a trip to the United Kingdom with Bob, Dolly enjoyed the full British experience, including Stonehenge,

The Faith of Dolly Parton

> 🦋 Pretend Dolly has asked you to write your own verse for this song. What would you add based on your own uphill climb? How would you compare this song to some of the Psalms in the Bible?

Dear God,

I sometimes struggle to keep trusting you when my life seems to turn upside down. I can't understand why you allow certain things to happen or how they fit into your plans, which I know are good because you are good. During these dark times, shine the light of your love within me. Give me hope and remind me of your promise to never leave me or forsake me.

Amen.

Divine Dose of Dolly

I am the light of the world. Whoever follows me will never walk in darkness, but will have the light of life.
   JOHN 8:12

🦋 What has been the hardest or most painful season of your life? How did you get through it? What role did your faith play in sustaining you and helping you come out of it?

🦋 How do you usually handle disappointment in your life? What losses are you carrying that you still need to grieve? How have these losses and disappointments affected your relationship with God? What do you need to tell him or ask him?

Listen to Dolly sing "I'll Keep Climbing" before answering the following questions.

🦋 How well does this song express your own struggle to keep climbing after walking through the valleys of life?

The Faith of Dolly Parton

Dolly at the Pure & Simple 7th Annual Gift Of Music at The Ryman Auditorium, 2015.

I suspect Dolly has learned to pray with the Psalmist, "I remain confident of this: I will see the goodness of the Lord in the land of the living. Wait for the Lord; be strong and take heart and wait for the Lord" (Psalm 27:13–14). Through these hard times she's revealed, as well as the ones she has kept private and close to her heart, Dolly has trusted God to shine through the shadows and lead her back into his light.

condition again. She committed to a healthier lifestyle and lost weight—about twenty pounds. She reached out to reconnect with old friends and reunited with family members. And she focused on being grateful for the overabundance of blessings in her life.

Dolly said she knew it would be a sin not to enjoy and appreciate the success God had given her. While she knew she might still face hard times and painful emotions, she committed to working at being happy. She recognized that it takes as much effort to be miserable as it does to be content and decided to make sure her focus and her faith remained fixed on God's goodness. In her book *Dream More*, based on her commencement speech to the graduating class at the University of Tennessee in 2009, Dolly shares her secrets for working at happiness: "Love what you do. Like yourself. Enjoy other people: their company, their ideas, their personalities. Keep a good spiritual grip on things. Always pray for understanding and acceptance."[6]

Wise advice from someone who has more spiritual depth than she's often given credit for—especially considering the struggles she's faced and the hard-fought battles she's won. Health crises, surgeries, binge eating, weight gain, depression, suicidal thoughts, family conflicts, sibling rivalry, personal betrayals, failed projects, and lawsuits based on false accusations. Dolly has dealt with them all, and through her faith in God has not allowed any of them to defeat her or snuff out the light in her soul.

But she wasn't going to sink back into her previous pit of despair without a fight.

With the paparazzi relentlessly hovering and reporting, the trial lasted twelve days and required both Fonda and Dolly to take the witness stand. Fortunately, the jury deliberated less than thirty minutes and announced a verdict in Dolly's favor. The court awarded her the legal and court costs, which had added up to a considerable sum. After the plaintiffs filed for a retrial (claiming Dolly used her star power to charm the jury), which was denied, they had the nerve to ask Dolly if she'd record some of their songs.

Even though she won the case, Dolly found the experience embarrassing and humiliating. As a creative artist who takes the hard work of songwriting very seriously, she hated for anyone to consider that she would ever steal someone else's work. And even though she knew this couple had no basis for their claim, it's hard to know how a jury might perceive the situation.

Bouncing Back

Dolly bounced back from this low point in her life, and she came back stronger than ever. She began writing new songs, mindful of the pain that so many people feel in the midst of life's struggles. She began dreaming new and bigger dreams, finally taking action on one she'd held for a while, with Dollywood as the result. And she made up her mind to never let herself get into the same kind of

Bumps in the Road

There are often bumps in the road even after you turn a corner. Emerging out of her dark night, Dolly's transition back to her former vibrant life was not easy, to say the least. After laying low and regaining her physical and emotional strength, she felt well enough to try the movies again, determined this time to control as much of the process as possible.

The result was *Rhinestone*, costarring Sylvester Stallone as a New York cabbie who agrees to a far-fetched plan by Dolly's character to transform him into a country music star. Stallone and Dolly have often commented on how much they enjoyed working with one another, but the film pleased neither the critics nor their fans. Despite her integral involvement in the production process, Dolly couldn't prevent numerous problems with the final product. The movie bombed.

Shortly after the disappointments of *Rhinestone*, Dolly encountered an even more troubling problem: a lawsuit from a couple in California claiming Dolly's hit song "9 to 5," which had received an Oscar nomination in addition to topping the charts, had been plagiarized from them. The details of their case seem dubious to me—alleging that Jane Fonda actually heard their song and passed it along to Dolly—but were apparently strong enough to go to trial. With legal filings and the trial hanging over her for weeks, Dolly had to overcome yet another obstacle.

longer had the energy to fight back. I thought of ways I could do it that would look like an accident, ensuring my family would receive my life insurance, and places where my wife and children would not be the first to find me.

To be honest, I'm not quite sure what broke my depression other than time and the constant love of my wife, children, and a few close friends. As the one-year anniversary of Daddy's death approached, I finally gave in to Dotti's now urgent request that I see a counselor and be open to antidepressant medication should I need it. Unable to bear the thought of leaving my children fatherless, I agreed.

It took time, but I was blessed to work with a counselor who quickly got me and what I was going through. He required me to have a thorough checkup, where my doctor prescribed Wellbutrin, which proved effective. The medication along with weekly therapy allowed me to face my demons and deal with the darkness inside. I started going back to church too, tentatively at first, but then in a way that felt like coming home. Despite all the pain, I knew God cared and had protected me and remained present with me, Word made flesh, his light shining in my darkness.

I knew I had a future and a hope and a lot of life left to live.

I had a wife to love and kids to raise and future grandkids to spoil.

And I had a lot of books yet to write.

before I did, but I couldn't talk about it with her or with anyone. I feared if I confronted it head-on, the darkness raging inside my heart would consume me, annihilate me, destroy me.

Part of it had to do with my own mortality, ironically enough. With my father's passing, I took his place on the generational front line, facing the inevitable as every human does. No matter how young and healthy I might be, no matter that I had lost weight and was actually in the best shape of my life from hiking and bike riding, my body would eventually fail. Approaching my fortieth birthday didn't help any.

The other half of my depression emerged from the glaring realization that I had spent most of my life trying to get my father's attention and attempting to please him. While he was hard on me in many ways, he also idolized me, setting me up to be the good son, the best version of himself that he could never attain. Meeting my previously unknown half brother, one who shared our father's first and last name with me, only reinforced this feeling. For whatever reasons, my father refused his responsibility to father this son who bore his name. As a result, I was his namesake's redemption, my father's do-over, his legitimate son who would make him proud.

Considering the many blessings in my life then, I'm ashamed to admit that I considered taking my own life. The despair weighed on me, pressing down and crushing me, squeezing my chest until I couldn't breathe and no

But this sensitivity also has a downside, a dark side, a shadow side.

It's why I felt pulled under by a churning riptide after my father died.

It's why, like Dolly, I considered ending my life.

Scars and Souvenirs

One of the hardest things to pack was my collection of the dozen or so journals I've kept sporadically over most of my adult life. I knew better than to flip through them; I knew I'd be pulled under the powerful current of old fears and feelings, but I couldn't help myself. Those words are a part of me, scars and souvenirs of my life and how I've lived it, processed it, and reflected on it. But as I randomly opened one filled notebook after another, I was embarrassed by the moodiness, the adolescence, the melodrama. There's evidence of my faith there too, but much of it was shaking my fist at God rather than holding his hand or resting in his arms.

Looking at the entries from the year after my father died, I was alarmed at the intensity of my pain—I couldn't handle it and instead usually felt numb, detached, withdrawn. I was in graduate school then and somehow managed to keep functioning, but there was a sharp divide within. I was going through the motions, but I wasn't sure why or what difference it made. Dotti, a trained counselor, recognized the symptoms of my depression when I saw it, validated the following year when the two renounced their vows, married, and moved away.

I was always asking myself, "What if?" when I'd see people going about their daily routines. What if Brother Bob started speaking French from the pulpit of the First Baptist Church this Sunday? What if a bank robber rushed into the First Federal branch on the country highway? What if our underdog junior varsity basketball team miraculously beat our biggest rival and made it to the state tourney? What if my daddy stopped drinking and came to my basketball games? What if there were life on Mars?

These speculations explain why I loved stories, especially mysteries, so much as a kid. There were all these questions and possibilities revolving around one big conflict or problem, and the hero used his mind to figure out the solution. After all, what is life if not one big mystery, a journey to be lived by faith?

My sponge-like imagination is why I ended up majoring in English and writing poems to capture the unique experience of a moment, an image, an event. It's why my favorite passage in Scripture comes from the beginning of John's gospel: "In the beginning was the Word, and the Word was with God, and the Word was God. . . . Through him all things were made. . . . In him was life, and that life was the light of all mankind. The light shines in the darkness, and the darkness has not overcome it. . . . The Word became flesh and made his dwelling among us" (John 1:1, 3–5, 14).

The Faith of Dolly Parton

The key ring from the first car I owned. A copy of the first poem I got published, "Barbershop," a free-verse portrait of my first haircut in my small hometown. Our engagement announcement clipped from the Sunday newspaper; I search the smiling eyes of the happy couple, my wife leaning on my shoulder. A baby blanket from one of the kids—I honestly don't know which one, although I'm sure my wife would—with little pastel stars, moons, and planets. Our Christmas card from a couple years ago with our three beautiful young adults smiling amidst the holiday lights of downtown Chicago.

I'm a sentimental man, and the older I get, the less I care who knows it. I've worked hard much of my life to hide my sensitivity, a word I've never particularly liked, based on the way people said it when I was growing up. "Don't be so sensitive, boy," my daddy said to me at my granddaddy's funeral. "Put those tears away and be tough—for your mama's sake." I was ten years old.

This sensitivity, though, this awareness of details and people and moments, has also served as the engine for my imagination. Growing up, I was always in my head, wondering about crazy things, like what it was like for the rooster tethered to a stake in the ground beside our barn to see the grass and trees and sky all around him but remain unable to explore it. Or what did my teacher, the pretty young nun, really think of Father Mark, the handsome young priest new to the parish? Too young to label romantic attraction or sexual tension, I still knew it closer walk with God. He had not abandoned her. He was with her the entire time, holding her close.

Dolly had discovered firsthand the truth described by Paul in his letter to the Christians in Rome: "I am convinced that nothing can ever separate us from God's love. Neither death nor life, neither angels nor demons, neither our fears for today nor our worries about tomorrow—not even the powers of hell can separate us from God's love" (Romans 8:38, NLT).

Unlocking the Past

I love Dolly's openness, even about the hard times in her life. It not only reveals a deeper dimension of her faith, but it also reminds us that everyone, sooner or later, faces their own uphill climb out of the valley of depression, doubt, and despair. Dolly's battle and the closer relationship she forged with God coming out of it comforted me as I reflected on many bittersweet memories while packing up my office in our house.

One of the reasons moving is so hard, at least for me, is because of all the emotions that come rushing out every time you open a closet, lift a box lid, or sort through a drawer. All the feelings attached to particular items from those different milestones and seasons in your life cannot be thrown away or simply packed, taped, and put on a shelf. Each one holds a story, like a message in a bottle tossed into the sea of memory so long ago and now washed ashore.

she remembered the handgun she kept in her nightstand in case of a break-in. Suddenly, she considered ending it all—having something right in front of her that could bring about the permanent end to her suffering.

Later in a dramatic interview in *Ladies' Home Journal* (June 1986), Dolly revealed to journalist Cliff Jahr that she actually picked up her gun, held it and stared at it in her hand, when suddenly she heard Popeye, the little dog she and Carl both loved, clattering into the room. "The tap-tap-tap of his paws jolted me back to reality," she shared. Dolly believes God used Popeye to intervene and break her out of such a terrible mind-set in that moment.[4]

While that incident was certainly a turning point, it didn't entirely break the grip of her depression. It did remind her, though, that she had always intended to read the Bible straight through from cover to cover. So that's what she started doing. From Genesis to the Gospels to Revelation, she searched for answers, and through the process of reading God's Word, Dolly found her lines of divine communication opening once again. The clouds began lifting from her spirit.

She began hearing God again and knew that he was hearing her prayers. Then she began feeling like herself again. She woke up one day and realized "life goes on whether you feel like being a part of it or not."[5] Dolly's dark night of the soul had ended, and dawn was breaking once more. Feeling lighter and more inspired than ever before, Dolly experienced a deepening of her faith and a usually paired up to make sure no one was forgotten. Baby Larry was to have been Dolly's sibling to help care for, so losing him seemed even more painful and personal. This loss led to her first crisis of faith as she struggled to make sense of it all. It took a little time, but Dolly came to terms with his death, and perhaps death in general, realizing that death is hardest for those of us left behind.

But those early struggles must have paled in comparison to the myriad of losses Dolly experienced as an adult. With so much of her life seemingly in shreds, she couldn't understand where God was and why he was allowing her to go through so much pain and despair. In her autobiography, she wrote, "I had never felt alone before. I had always had God. I had always thought of him as a friend, my constant fortress, my loving father. I had always heard the voice of God guiding me along my way through life. Now pain and anguish ripped at my heart, fear and anguish clouded my mind. I could not hear him. I wondered if even he had forsaken me. I questioned God. I argued with him."[3]

With so many huge, existential questions clouding her mind and taunting her heart, Dolly wondered if she would ever have answers—or any peace of mind—again. Death held the appeal of not having to worry about any of it and finally experiencing freedom from all the pain, despair, and heartache in her life. Such thoughts and feelings led Dolly to a moment when she contemplated suicide as a very real option. Sitting upstairs in her bedroom,

Crisis of Faith

It's not surprising that in the midst of such turmoil, Dolly also experienced a crisis of faith. When things are going well, it's relatively easy to thank God for your blessings. But when everything's taken away and you feel disoriented by the depths of your losses, it's hard to believe God is still good and that he still cares about your well-being.

Dolly is no different than the rest of us. This painful season of loss was not the first time, of course, she had ached with grief and questioned God's purposes. When Dolly was a girl, her mother almost died of spinal meningitis. Burning up with fever, Avie Lee was rushed to the hospital after a home visit from Dr. Thomas, the local doctor who had delivered Dolly. Their family knew it was serious if someone was taken to the hospital, and they worried they might lose their beloved mama.

Dolly remembers her grandma Rena, Dolly's mother's mama, sitting up all night, clutching her Bible and praying fervently, "Whatsoever ye shall ask in prayer, believing, ye shall receive" (Matthew 21:22, KJV). The next morning, Mrs. Parton's fever broke. Having survived through the long night, Mama Parton recovered and went on to live until she was eighty, seeing and enjoying much of Dolly's success before passing away in 2003.

In addition to this scare, Dolly had also lost a baby brother, Larry, who died the day after his birth. In their family the older kids helped take care of the younger ones, some colleagues involved with the music for her movie with Burt were fired and others hired, which Dolly feared she may have triggered unintentionally. To top it all off, she was also forced to deal with family members who suddenly seemed resentful and jealous of her success, eager to prove their own musical abilities, with or without Dolly's help. As a full-fledged star, Dolly also attracted threats from would-be stalkers, including a particularly persistent and dangerous one who caused her to cancel the rest of her tour during this troubling season.

It was all too much for her.

Her marriage to Carl remained rock solid; however, Dolly felt protective of him, aware he was already anxious about her physical problems. She didn't feel free to share all of her other worries with him for fear of burdening him further. So she kept it all inside and began to withdraw. She would binge eat, feel worse, and stay in bed all day, cancelling concerts and appearances, which only caused new legal entanglements.

But Dolly didn't care. Everything in her life she cared the most about had all crashed at the same time—her health, her future, her friendships, her family. In an interview a few years later, Dolly revealed, "It was bad. It was devastating to be in that depressed state of mind. For about six months there I woke up every morning feeling dead." She felt like the joyful, daring dreamer inside her had died, leaving her "a fat, disillusioned, hopeless woman."[2]

put her costar in hospital, for which she apologized and asked forgiveness. By her own account she was the heaviest she had ever been in her life, calling herself a "real porker."[1]

Looking back, she laughs about that story, but her experience at the time was no laughing matter. Her weight gain resulted from emotional eating as Dolly faced a perfect storm of emotional and physical issues colliding. What she calls "female problems," had wreaked havoc with her hormones and emotions. Finally, performing a concert in Indianapolis, she nearly collapsed due to internal abdominal hemorrhaging and was rushed to the hospital.

When medication failed to get her body's gynecological issues under control, she was forced to have several surgical procedures, which ended her ability to conceive and bear children. This was devastating for her. In addition to dealing with the healing and recovery process of her body, she also had to come to terms with and accept this life-changing news.

It was a stormy time in both her personal and professional relationships. Her best friend Judy Ogle and other close team members were involved in life circumstances of their own, which pulled them away from Dolly, who found herself more alone than usual. During this time, she also experienced a personal betrayal by someone very close to her, which left her shattered.

In addition, she worried about her reputation because

best little brothel in Texas. The movie was based on a hit Broadway musical, with the film keeping some songs but giving Dolly room to contribute new ones.

Cast with popular star Burt Reynolds, Dolly hoped to enjoy filming with him as much as she'd loved working with Jane Fonda and Lily Tomlin in her first movie experience. Instead, she suffered through the exact opposite of the happy set and camaraderie of *9 to 5*. Apparently, the film's production team had already lost battles with studio heads over keeping key members of the Broadway team. And major stakeholders were unhappy with the transition from stage to screen long before Dolly joined the cast.

While Dolly has always said that she and Burt got along fine, the dynamic with her costar was strained by his own problems, including the recent, high-profile breakup with his *Smokey and the Bandit* partner, Sally Field. It was also strained, according to Dolly's account in her autobiography, by her weight gain. Not only was she not feeling good about herself, but one particular scene at the end of the filming accentuated it.

The script called for Burt's character to pick up Miss Mona and carry her through a doorway. Numerous takes were required, and each time Burt grunted and groaned a little louder. They finally concluded the shots needed, but apparently a couple weeks later Burt underwent an operation to repair a double hernia. Though it was a pre-existing condition, Dolly feared she may have she'll be laid off by her employer. But if Dolly is anything, she is wonderfully human. She knows about suffering heartache, facing disappointment, and enduring pain. She worries about her husband, struggles with an aging body (despite not appearing to get older), and wants the best for her family. No matter how successful she's become, she has remained grounded by her roots and humility—but also by her pain.

As positive as she is, and as successful as she became at an early age, Dolly has still faced struggles that threatened to consume her. She has channeled her experiences into her music, keenly aware of the kind of legacy she wants to leave. And with her typical honesty and candor, Dolly has shared the intensity of her battles publicly, particularly her depression in the midst of a major health crisis. After coming out of it, she even confessed that she was tempted to consider something that had never crossed her mind before.

She reached a point where she wondered if she wanted to go on living.

Highs and Lows

Dolly hit this low point after reaching new heights of stardom. After the phenomenal success of *9 to 5*, she chose another movie vehicle that seemed custom-made for both her larger-than-life persona and her gifted musical abilities: the role of Miss Mona, the owner and operator of the

CHAPTER 8

Shine through the Shadows

We all need to have hope that there's something bigger than we are.
   DOLLY PARTON

Despite walking in the light and living in the spotlight, Dolly has been through some dark times. In fact, we probably wouldn't trust her faith and connect to her music if she hadn't been through the valley of shadows. You can only celebrate reaching the mountaintop if you can look back and see all you had to go through to get there. Or as Dolly often says, "If you want the rainbow, you have to put up with the rain."

We might be tempted to think stars like Dolly don't struggle with the same issues that you and me—and most people—face on a regular basis. True, she might not be worrying about paying her mortgage this month or if

The Faith of Dolly Parton

🦋 Do you believe we tend to romanticize our past and the hardships we've endured? Based on the words in this song, which Dolly indeed wrote, how do you think she regards her early struggles in light of her present success?

Dear God,

I know you have a plan for my life and that you have a place where I belong here on earth—as well as an eternal home in heaven. For both the good and bad things that I recall, I thank you for the place where I grew up, the place I'm from. Help me to carry the best parts of this place with me wherever I go, showing hospitality by opening my home to others and welcoming them to share it.

Amen.

Let Your Roots Keep You Grounded

Divine Dose of Dolly

Humble yourselves before the Lord, and he will lift you up.
   JAMES 4:10

🦋 How connected do you feel to your roots, to the people and places that shaped you while growing up? Do you harbor mostly positive memories and associations or negative ones? Or is it a mixture of both?

🦋 How have the early years of your life led you to where you are now? What have you taken with you from childhood that has helped you on your journey? What baggage do you need to release?

Listen to Dolly sing "My Tennessee Mountain Home" before answering the following questions.

🦋 What songs or pieces of music do you associate with the place you call home? How do they reflect your feelings about this place?

The Faith of Dolly Parton

"What are you talking about? I thought I was born at the hospital here in Sewanee," I said, wondering if my mom, about to turn eighty and sharp as ever, was confused.

"That *is* the old hospital here," she said, smiling, before proceeding to tell me about the day I was born there a little over five decades earlier.

I didn't doubt her, but later I went to look at the building, did a little sleuthing online, and verified that Hodgson Hall is indeed the location of the old campus infirmary and local hospital. The new one, closer to the main highway and access to the interstate, was built years after I was born.

Unbelievable.

As it turned out, I was living only a football field away from the place where I entered the world, the building where my aunt Tommy served as head nurse for most of her career. Such close proximity seemed too conspicuous to be merely a coincidence. The house on Morgan's Steep welcomed me back to Tennessee with direct ties to my past on one side and a stunning, wide-open view of my future on the other. Its location seems incredibly symbolic—a divine coincidence that continues to encourage and inspire me during this season of transition, a promise bridging where I started with where I'm going, back to my Tennessee roots.

purchasing another, we decided to see if we could find a place to rent in Sewanee. In addition to providing a transitional home, a rental there would also allow us to check out the area and see if we liked it as much as we thought we would, without the more permanent commitment of buying a home right away.

Our options were limited, largely because Sewanee is a university town, so most rentals were already occupied by students and faculty. Fortunately, however, we discovered an opportunity to rent a house on campus, a charming old farmhouse almost 150 years old. With double porches, uneven floors, and a cut-stone fireplace custom built from local quarries, the place has proven to be a haven for me to write this book.

Located on a quiet residential street, the house is only a few hundred yards away from a local landmark, Morgan's Steep, a trailhead and overlook precariously perched on the stone lip of the mountain. From there, I look down into the valley below and see the swell of hills rolling on either side, a gorgeous view no matter the weather or season. It's hard to believe such dramatic beauty is so close to the house, a three-minute walk out the front door. Hardly a day goes by that I don't stroll down to take in the sunset.

In the other direction, up the hill from this house we've rented, is one of the university's dormitories, Hodgson Hall. When my mother visited for the first time, she looked at the old three-story brownstone dorm and said, "You know that's where you were born, don't you?"

When others praise her, though, Dolly usually jokes and demurs into an aww-shucks attitude. She gives God the credit for her talent and for blessing her with such an abundance of opportunities. She doesn't brag or showboat or play the diva to the hilt like she's certainly entitled. Instead, she uses that talent to connect to people, to inspire them, to console them, to excite them and entertain them. And she uses the profits from her talented career to improve the lives of men, women, and children, not only in Tennessee but around the world.

No doubt, Dolly knows how to promote, to charm, and to maximize exposure for her next album, concert, movie, show, or other creative endeavor. But she also uses those as opportunities for a greater good than just the advancement of her career or strokes for her ego. She uses them to remind people what matters most in life—living with purpose, loving with abandon, laughing whenever possible, and looking ahead for where God wants to take you next.

All without forgetting where you started.

Bridging Past and Present

As I finish writing this book, our house has not yet sold. We remain optimistic, though, because the market in our area is quite strong. In fact, everyone told us to anticipate selling quickly and to have a plan in place for the transition. Knowing we have to sell our current home before

Let Your Roots Keep You Grounded

William Smokey Robinson, Andrew Lloyd Webber, Dolly Parton, President George W. Bush, Laura Bush, Steven Spielberg, and Zubin Mehta at the Kennedy Center Honors dinner, 2006

I'm far from an expert, but I do have graduate degrees in literature and creative writing, and I find many of her songs just as innovative, compelling, and poetic as many of the contemporary poets I've studied. She knows how to tell a story, which details to include, how to bring a character's perspective to life, and the natural expressions people use when they talk. She utilizes form and function, repetition and alliteration, simile and metaphor. Dolly may not win the Nobel Prize for Literature like her peer Bob Dylan (then again, she might!), but her work takes the roots of her musical heritage—Gospel, bluegrass, folk, and country—and blends them into new hybrids that cross genres and appeal to a wide and diverse fan base.

The Faith of Dolly Parton

Without a doubt, Dolly naturally had to get used to being the center of attention and likely enjoyed being there much of the time—especially considering how she had to compete for her parents' attention with her many siblings. But for all her accomplishments and the accolades she's received, Dolly refuses to think too highly of herself. She's often said how much she values direct, look-me-in-the-eye honesty, a standard she applies to herself as well.

Throughout her career, Dolly has repeatedly said she's really not a great singer and that her voice is just fair. She doesn't consider herself an actress, merely more of a performer, an entertainer in a role similar enough to her own experiences to portray it faithfully. Nonetheless, with over a hundred million records sold, dozens of hit singles, and a room full of awards, she's undeniably gifted. She's been chosen as a recipient of the prestigious Kennedy Center Honors, has nine Grammy Awards, and has twice been nominated for an Academy Award.

The ability of which Dolly is most proud is likely her songwriting. Dolly's lyrics and contagious melodies may indeed be her greatest artistic achievement. While she hasn't written all of her hits, she has definitely composed the majority of them. And with over three thousand songs copyrighted, she has plenty to draw on and doesn't show signs of slowing down any time soon. She just recently released her first children's album, *I Believe in You*, the forty-fourth studio album of her storied career, with proceeds going to her amazing Imagination Library program.

garden, a grape arbor, a small apple orchard, and a *koi* pond with huge goldfish swimming in it under a giant evergreen tree. To me it felt like the Garden of Eden! I had a statue giving me permission to pee outside, apples to eat, and fish to try and catch.

No wonder I wanted to move back to Sewanee.

Keep It Humble

My aunt Tommy was incredibly private and very humble. She didn't like people knowing her business or how much she did for others. Maybe that's another reason I admire Dolly. I see these same tendencies in her and the way she lives out her faith. Obviously, their lives are quite different, with Dolly's career inherently requiring her to be in the public eye so much of the time. But all the more reason that Dolly impresses me with the way she guards her private life, including her marriage to Carl, and separates it from her very public performing life. Some reporters have even faulted her for seeming so transparent in interviews yet not really divulging anything they didn't already know.

Dolly has consistently displayed a humility that's remarkable for a star with such a long, varied, and incredibly successful career. She reflects the truths about humility—and the danger of pride—found in the Bible: "Humble yourselves before the Lord, and he will lift you up" (James 4:10). "When pride comes, then comes disgrace, but with humility comes wisdom" (Proverbs 11:2).

thick gold charm bracelet from her wrist, with charms from all the places she'd been. She read voraciously, mostly fiction, and depended on the Sunday *New York Times* as her ultimate source, because if it wasn't in the Times, then she didn't need to know it.

She had married late in life to my uncle Ross, a local widower, a veteran of World War I who worked at the town post office. They had no children together, and consequently Aunt Tommy had become like a second mother to her niece, my mom. As a nurse Tommy made good money, certainly by our family's standards in the area where we lived, and, like Dolly, was incredibly generous with it. She made sure my brother Barry and I had new school clothes every fall. She took my mother shopping in Nashville or Atlanta, buying her new dresses or cookware or whatever happened to strike her fancy. I suspect she influenced my parents' decision to send me to Catholic school, perhaps providing the monthly tuition payment during lean times.

Aunt Tommy was not only educated and worked as a professional, but she embraced the world and relished it on her terms. She loved beautiful things—colored glassware, classical music, handmade furniture—and her home on the brow of Sewanee Mountain remains one of the happiest places of my life. Her driveway ran for about a quarter mile through dense woods before opening to that incredible mountain vista. Behind her house, a fountain with a working replica of the famous *Manneken Pis* statue in Brussels welcomed you to a formal flower

Let Your Roots Keep You Grounded

1857 and still owned by a collection of dioceses of the Episcopal Church. Because its history is so entwined with the town, and because the university owns over thirteen thousand acres (the "domain" as it's known), it's simply called Sewanee by most people.

No, we're not Episcopal, and neither of us went to school there. Nonetheless, Sewanee, both the town and its campus, had always been a special place for me. My aunt Tommy, who was actually my grandfather's sister, lived there most of her life and worked as the head nurse for the small local hospital. Her real name was Zollie, but she didn't like it. "Doesn't the sound of it just freeze your blood?" she'd always say. With friends and family she preferred Tommy, a nickname appropriated from a teenage crush she'd had on a farmer boy by the same name.

She and Dolly would have bonded as kindred spirits had they ever met. Not because Aunt Tommy loved country music but simply because of her independent, quirky, standout, vibrant personality. She simply wasn't like the rest of my family—or anyone else I knew. Her sensibilities appealed to me as a boy who often feared being trapped in his small hometown for the rest of his life. She helped deliver me; that's why I was born in Sewanee.

A tall statuesque woman with a large bosom, Tommy wore dresses from fine stores in Atlanta or Nashville, she carried herself like a queen, and always looked put together in a classy yet natural way. She favored red lipstick, wore her dark silvery hair in a bun, and jangled a

The Faith of Dolly Parton

Tennessee. Since we had no deadline to hit—such as the start of a new job or the beginning of school for the kids—Dotti and I tried to take the pressure off each other. We made to-do lists and began chipping away at those things you put off doing for yourself but must do before selling your house to someone else. You know, patching the hole in the wall of my son's room, unclogging the dryer vent, replacing the light fixture in the hall that didn't match the others—those fun kinds of things.

Making progress on that front, we decided to drive to Tennessee, have a look around, and visit our families, informing them of our decision in as casual a way as possible. We knew they'd be excited, but neither of us wanted to feel pressured by their expectations either. We already had an area in mind, one easily within an hour of the town where my mother and brother lived and only a couple hours away from Dotti's family. This area perched along the edge of the Cumberland Plateau, low-lying mountains ramping up to the Appalachians and Smokies to the northeast.

The town where I was born, Sewanee, Tennessee, particularly intrigued us. For one thing, it's on a mountaintop surrounded by hills and other mountains, coves and valleys, with an abundance of the four seasons' natural beauty. The other thing uniquely appealing about Sewanee is the university there. Officially, it's The University of the South, a private four-year residential liberal arts college and graduate seminary established in depending on where we settled, close proximity to the many thriving cultural opportunities in Nashville.

It all just made sense.

Back Where I Started

Although we continued talking about it, the decision to move had seemingly been made. Dotti loved the idea of returning to Tennessee, aware just as I was that no matter where we moved, we'd be starting over once again, a strangeness compounded by the absence of the kids from our home. As we discussed the idea with each of our children, they understood and supported our decision. Still, each expressed, in their own individual way, a kind of sadness at the passing of this season of their lives.

One daughter whooped, another got a new tattoo, and our son wept, already feeling off-kilter by the vast openness of his future after graduation. We told them all that regular visits to our new home were mandatory, and that they were welcome to move with us—but only if they made that decision deliberately and not by default. I had felt guilty and more than a little selfish for uprooting the five of us a couple times already, a feeling I intended to relinquish with this move.

Although the big decision was out of the way, we were quickly overwhelmed by all that had to be done. Generally, we needed to sort and clear out a lifetime of stuff, prepare our house to sell, and find a place to land in

The Faith of Dolly Parton

But Colorado is so far away. One of the pluses of living in Michigan was our ability to drive to Tennessee in less than a day to visit our families. Dotti had been able to visit Knoxville frequently in the months leading to her father's death. She remained close with her sisters and brother who lived there. My mother still lived in Middle Tennessee as well as my brother and his family. Barry is my mother's son from her first marriage, and while he's almost ten years older than I am, he's the only brother I grew up knowing, as opposed to the new acquaintance with my same first name. I had always enjoyed our time together, especially in the past few years.

Our daughter in Colorado also warned us that things had changed considerably during the decade we had been away. A steady influx of new residents contributed to more highway congestion, retail growth, and shockingly high home prices. Although we joked about the legalization of pot being the causal factor, I knew that this new industry and its culture had indeed made an impact.

If we didn't move west, then our other logical option was to head south to Tennessee. In addition to having both of our families there, we knew old friends and familiarity with the region would make for an easier transition. The cost of living would be slightly cheaper than Michigan and considerably less than Colorado. Tennessee is one of the few remaining states without a state income tax. I would also have plenty of mountains, along with SEC college football (Go Vols!), real Southern barbeque, and,

Let Your Roots Keep You Grounded

I began facing the inevitable empty nest, knowing we had way too much nest for just the two of us. It was time to downsize and transition into our next season of life.

Dotti and I didn't feel old yet (well, most days at least), but we longed for a smaller place with less upkeep than our large home there in the woods near the Thornapple River. Besides, I'm blessed to be able to do what I do for a living—write and consult, most anywhere I can open my laptop. We had been in Michigan for almost ten years, and despite how many people we had grown to love there, we still longed for closer community.

Truth be told, I'd never felt like I belonged in the Wolverine State. Despite the acronym I'd learned in school to memorize the Great Lakes, HOMES (Huron, Ontario, Michigan, Erie, Superior), I hadn't found one there. For all their incredible beauty, the Great Lakes are not the Rockies or the Smokies. No matter how much I like lakes and rivers, beaches and shoreline, I *love* the mountains. I like their size, their constancy, their ever-changing seasonal moods. Hiking wooded trails, looking at neighboring peaks from a hard-won summit climb, breathing in crisp pine-scented air—that's where I feel at home.

With our oldest daughter living back in Colorado, my wife and I considered moving back there where we had so many happy memories of raising our family. And we still have good friends there with whom we've remained close. We're familiar with most areas of the Front Range and would know where to look for the kind of home we'd like.

Porter's show as well as her albums, Dolly and husband Carl bought a parcel of property, around seventy-five acres, outside of Nashville on which to build their dream home. Dolly not only made sure her parents had their own home onsite, she invited her youngest siblings to live with her and Carl. She wanted to provide them with the kind of lifestyle she longed for but never had as a child.

Since she and Carl had no biological children of their own, being surrogate parents to her younger siblings likely allowed Dolly to express her maternal side. As her brothers and sisters became adults, left the nest, and started families of their own, Dolly was delighted to spoil their children too. Feeling like their grandmother in a sense, but not wanting to take anything away from both sets of grandparents they actually had, Dolly came up with her own solution for what the kids would call her and Carl: "Aunt Granny and Uncle PeePaw."[5]

Making a Move

My desire to write this book exploring Dolly's faith and the ways she has inspired me throughout my life coincided, fittingly enough, with a longing to move back home to Tennessee. After moving my family to Grand Rapids for that big job I told you about, I honored my promise to my kids to remain there in Michigan at least until they finished high school. When our youngest, Jacob, graduated from Caledonia High School in 2017, my wife, Dotti, and career, but she didn't have to do what she did. In fact, I suspect a lesser person might have been tempted to lord her newfound success over everyone else, proving once and for all that she was the exceptional one among them. Not Dolly. Her natural generosity to those she loves, especially her supportive family, has kept her grounded. She vowed never to forget what it was like to go without, and she hasn't. She wants to use the blessings God has bestowed on her to bless others. "I always count my blessings far more than I ever count my money," Dolly said.[3] "Giving back has nothing to do with being rich."[4]

Here's another early example. It's telling that after "Coat of Many Colors" became a big hit in 1971, Dolly wanted to do something special for her mother, who obviously figures at the center of both the experience and the song it inspired. So Dolly went home to see her mama and told her she wanted to take her to Knoxville and buy her a mink coat to bring the moving memory of the little patchwork coat full circle. Her mother thanked her but wondered about the practicality of owning something as fancy as a mink coat, which would stick out like a peacock in a henhouse at church and in town. Mama Parton told Dolly to just give her the money her famous daughter would have spent on such an extravagant gift, and that's what Dolly did.

She never lost touch with her large, close-knit family, and in fact, eagerly shared her success with them. Once her star, and her bank account balances, began rising from them change how she saw herself, which was the way God saw her.

From an early age, however, Dolly refused to let her self-worth be determined by her circumstances. She maintained this belief even as her fame and fortune grew. Sure, she enjoyed the fruits of her success and bought a new Cadillac once she landed on Porter's show. And she obviously likes her clothes, jewelry, wigs, and all her glamorous accessories, none of which come cheap. But Dolly didn't let her wealth change the way she saw herself—or others; her view remained the same as it had always been. Consequently, she didn't feel compelled to hoard and acquire more money and possessions just for her own security and self-worth. If anything, she felt liberated to share with those around her, particularly her loved ones.

Dolly had made "a secret promise to God"[2] that once she hit it big, she would take care of her parents and siblings. Her first year with Porter, Dolly earned what seemed like a fortune to her at the time: $60,000. So Dolly surprised her family that Christmas with a home makeover. With the help of her other adult siblings, Dolly coaxed her parents to leave the house for a day while she and her helpers brought in new furniture, carpet, and curtains for every room. She created a frilly, feminine bedroom for her younger sisters still at home, wanting them to have a much better life than she'd had at their age.

What's striking is that right out of the gate, Dolly was thinking of others. Yes, she had hit the jackpot with her

her with the love, beauty, and faith so vital to her personality and her artistry.

She never wanted to leave Sevier County, her Tennessee mountain home, or her family and friends—so, as she has often said, she takes them with her wherever she goes. Divinely destined for a life that pulled her not only across the country but also around the world, Dolly found ways to stay connected to where she started. This connection is reflected throughout Dollywood, as one astute writer pointed out after visiting the park:

"She has defied critics, stayed true to herself and turned stereotype into power. Nearly every corner of Dollywood reflects that. One can see both a replica of her childhood cabin and the inside of her tour bus, her ragged childhood clothes and her glittery gowns. She embraces her roots in a way that never seems manipulated but only serves to make her entire narrative stronger."[1]

Better to Give

As special as she considered herself to be while growing up, however, Dolly never claimed to be better than those around her. In her "Coat of Many Colors" song and depicted in the movie based on it, Dolly makes the distinction she obviously learned at an early age: who you are is not defined by what's on the outside but rather on the inside. Growing up poor and being teased and taunted about it by other kids and classmates, Dolly did not let memoirs, and novels where characters look for something they once had, or thought they had, but can't reclaim. This journey to reconcile the past with the present seems especially common among Southern writers during the twentieth century. In addition to Wolfe, I think of William Faulkner and Eudora Welty, Flannery O'Connor and Harper Lee, Walker Percy and Peter Taylor, and many others.

But they never met Dolly Parton.

In her typically exceptional way, Dolly shows us that you *can* go home again—if you're willing to remain humble, honest about who you are, and a good steward of the legacy entrusted to you.

Dolly has become practically synonymous with East Tennessee and the Great Smoky Mountains. And it's more than the eponymous title of Dollywood, more than the replica of the two-room cabin where she was born and the personal history immortalized in that place. It's her personal sense of pride and belonging, her affection and personal attachment, her appreciation for the natural beauty there, and her love and respect for its people.

Many celebrities work hard to escape where they started, the small towns and working-class families which they outgrew on their journey to Hollywood, New York, Nashville, and beyond. Others try to maintain their roots but end up finding little in common with those they once knew and loved in childhood. Dolly, on the other hand, never wanted to leave behind the vital roots that nurtured

CHAPTER 7

Let Your Roots Keep You Grounded

I try to always remember where I came from, who I am and why I wanted to do this to start with. It was not to get away from my family. It was not because I wasn't proud of my home, that I wanted to leave it. I just wanted to take the Smoky Mountains wherever I went.
                    DOLLY PARTON

It's not always easy to go home. In fact, Thomas Wolfe, a native of Asheville, North Carolina, just on the other side of the Smokies, famously wrote a novel reminding us *You Can't Go Home Again.* At one time or another in our lives, though, most of us experience both the longing and the struggle to belong, to feel connected to the place and people from where we came.

Many writers have explored this theme in stories,

The Faith of Dolly Parton

🦋 How do the words to this song encourage you to press on and keep risking in pursuit of your dreams? Can you relate to the freedom of the eagle's flight Dolly describes? What stands between you and your own clear, blue morning?

Dear God,

I give you thanks for all the many blessings of my life. Give me wisdom to be the best steward I can be with all you've entrusted to me. Grant me the courage to trust you and step out in faith even when it doesn't seem to make sense. Calm my fears with your presence and your peace that passes understanding. May all that I do be for your glory.

Amen.

Baby Steps toward a Leap of Faith

Divine Dose of Dolly

For we live by faith, not by sight.
2 CORINTHIANS 5:7

🦋 What risks have you taken in your life to further your dreams? What do you consider your greatest risk? How has it worked out for you? If you had it to do over again, would you risk differently? Why or why not?

🦋 What frightens you more about taking big risks—what you'll lose in the process or what you'll gain? What added burdens of responsibility have you encountered after taking a big risk? How have you handled it?

Listen to Dolly sing "Light of a Clear Blue Morning" before answering the following questions. Keep in mind that Dolly wrote this song following her departure from Porter Wagoner, inspired when she was driving and literally saw the clouds clear and the sun come shining through.

🦋 What emotions stirred in you while listening to Dolly share this song? Why? How does the song's tempo and melody contribute to these feelings?

remaining where you are. Empowered by your faith in God, you, too, can find the courage to risk and pursue your wildest dreams. And should you need further inspiration, I highly recommend a visit to Dollywood!

Baby Steps toward a Leap of Faith

So I quit my job.

Soon I had more work as an editor, collaborative writer, and book doctor than I had ever dreamed possible. I was blessed with opportunities to travel to Thailand and Cambodia where I worked on the novelization of a feature film that an old friend from graduate school was producing. There I got to meet Academy Award winner Mira Sorvino (a handful of us went bowling and sang karaoke with her!), tour the amazing ruins of Angkor Wat, and write a story about the heartbreaking issue of human trafficking.

By the grace of God, I've seen my writing dreams come true and traveled to some amazing places around the world—Australia, Italy, Ireland, and Haiti to name a few—and worked with bestselling authors, celebrated athletes, country music stars, and spent the day with a former US president. Not bad for a boy who was the first to go to college in his family!

I've been working this way for over seven years now, and while there are certainly lean times, I've been blessed to support my family and enjoy the freedom that comes from managing my own schedule and writing for a living. Best of all, I've gotten to write a book about one of my favorite people of all time, this very book that you're reading right now!

I'm not the only one who has been inspired by Dolly's example to risk big. No matter where you are in life, don't settle for security over satisfaction or resign yourself to

The Faith of Dolly Parton

It took three months of praying before I sensed God leading me to take the risk, accept the offer, and move my family to Grand Rapids, Michigan, where Zondervan is based. It took three years there, however, for me to realize God had an even bigger leap in mind. After ten years in corporate publishing, I could renew my contract for a couple more years, which was the logical thing to do, or I could follow my heart and do something a little crazy: go out on my own as a freelance writer, editor, and consultant.

I wanted to be home more. I knew my family had suffered because of my long hours and frequent travel. And I wanted to write more. I felt drained by my less-than-favorite tasks such as managing, marketing, and budgeting instead of pursuing my passions for books and writing. There was little time and no emotional energy for loving my wife and kids, now teenagers, or being directly involved in writing and making books that mattered.

As I pondered my decision, I didn't have to think about what Dolly would do—I had already watched my favorite star take risk after risk. Dolly would have simply laughed that silver-chime laugh of hers and asked me, "What are you waiting on, sugar?"

My wife, Dotti, agreed wholeheartedly. "What's the worst that can happen?" she said. "You try it and it doesn't work out. We sell the house and downsize. You get another job. I'll get a job. As long as our family is together, it will all fall into place. But you need to do this. It's time."

Baby Steps toward a Leap of Faith

I have faced moments when I risked security to follow my heart and chase a dream. I found myself at the edge of such a dilemma after ten years working in corporate publishing. By that time, I'd advanced higher than I'd ever imagined, becoming senior vice president and trade book publisher of arguably the most successful Christian publishing company, Zondervan. It was a dream job, and yet I longed for more.

Owned by Rupert Murdoch's News Corp within the renowned HarperCollins publishing family, Zondervan published so many writers I admired, respected, and revered and had made publishing history with the megabestselling *The Purpose Driven Life*. After being pursued for the job, I expressed my gratitude at such an opportunity but also my reluctance to leave Colorado. By that time our kids were all in school, with our oldest just starting high school. Our family loved living in Colorado Springs with Pikes Peak looming to the west above us like a solemn sentinel. We enjoyed the outdoor lifestyle as well as a strong, loving community of friends from work, school, and church.

But the executive conducting the search proved both persistent and persuasive. Having recently turned forty, I knew that this was the career opportunity of a lifetime. I would be in charge of a team acquiring, editing, launching, and marketing over a hundred titles a year. I would get to meet and work with some of the most amazing, talented, faith-filled people on the planet.

believe she grew up in a place like this?" She snapped a couple pictures before extending her hand for a selfie of the two of them.

"This is just like where my PawPaw grew up," said the man, dressed in jeans, a camo jacket, and a UT cap. "No toilet, no lights. Dolly knows what it was like just like him—he always said it made him tougher." His East Tennessee accent seemed more pronounced than his companion's.

"Well, it worked for Dolly, that's for sure," said the woman as they turned to exit.

Totally subjective and about as unscientific as you can get, but from what I heard and saw that day, I concluded that there's something about Dolly to which people relate, whether it's a sense of her sincerity, her authenticity, or her humanity (she not only pees like the rest of us, she once revealed on NBC's TODAY show her ritual before every performance: praying and then peeing, in that order). More likely, it's all of those qualities and more. It's the way she wears her glittery outfits and big hair without forgetting the little girl in the patchwork coat who grew up in a two-room cabin in the Smoky Mountains.

It's the way she's created a theme park that honors both.

A huge risk that has clearly paid off.

Chasing My Dream

I've never taken a risk as big as starting a theme park named after myself (Dudleywood? Dudleyland?), but back out, pausing at the miniature oven to say, "Dolly loves to cook and did all the cooking on her tours right here, using only these two burners."

"But what a couple of *big* burners they are!" said a would-be comedian, who looked like a biker except for his North Face jacket.

We all laughed at this joke that Dolly herself might have made had she been there.

Next I took in a show featuring Christmas music performed by a bluegrass band, happy to tap along to "Joy to the World" and bask once again in the winter sun. From there I wandered uphill to the Craftsman's Valley, browsed through several shops, smelling soaps and scented candles along the way. As the afternoon wore on, the park continued to fill—more families, many with small children, older couples, probably quite a few locals, a couple church youth groups, and plenty of regular people enjoying a Saturday at Dollywood.

I vividly recalled seeing the replica of the cabin in which Dolly grew up, and it was as dramatically small and sparse as I remembered. I had heard her say somewhere that constructing and furnishing the two-room facsimile of her childhood home had ironically cost over a million dollars. As I stood looking through plexiglass at an old SPAM can near the woodstove in the little kitchen, a couple in their midthirties walked up.

"Hard to believe, isn't it?" said the woman, pushing back her hoodie for a better, unobstructed view. "Can you

The Faith of Dolly Parton

Once inside the park, I ate some hot cinnamon bread from the Grist Mill, then wandered over to "Chasing Rainbows," the museum providing an overview of Dolly's life with plenty of artifacts, sparkly dresses, gold records, and audio-video opportunities to learn more and to listen to her music. Having completed so much research already, I enjoyed spending over an hour there before heading outside to see the big tour bus parked outside. Lines were relatively short, and since I was alone, the park attendant discreetly moved me up to complete the next viewing party. About eight of us then crowded onto the bus Dolly had used for fifteen years when touring.

I had been on such buses before, had even traveled on them a couple of times when working on book projects with touring performers. The layout was what you'd expect: a tiny kitchen, sitting area, bathroom, bunks lining either side, and Dolly's bedroom in the back. Standing shoulder to shoulder, it was hard not to hear the couples around me whispering. One woman in a floral sweatshirt took a picture of the tiny bathroom with her phone camera before turning to her husband and giggling, "That's where Dolly used to pee!"

Her companion, a very tall gentleman with a tanned face and silver crewcut rolled his eyes, clearly unamused, and said, "Dolly has to go just like the rest of us."

"That's what I love about her," the woman said. "Dolly is not afraid to be just like the rest of us."

Very telling.

Our hostess finished telling us her spiel and led us

Baby Steps toward a Leap of Faith

know nothin' 'bout Dolly Parton. I'll bet you all her money she'd rather be right here in this park singin' and meetin' people than traipsin' 'round some fancy store."

The daughter ignored him just as our shuttle ride ended and we were deposited at the park entrance. But I was intrigued by what I'd heard, especially the father's perception and assumptions about Dolly.

My trip to Dollywood, 2017

The Faith of Dolly Parton

was afraid if I didn't keep moving, someone might throw some lights on me!

Other than the twinkling lights and holiday décor, I didn't know what to expect. I wondered if it would be as crowded as my past summer visits (almost) and if it had changed much (definitely larger). Most of all, I wanted to know what drew people to this place. With roughly three million visitors a year now, who comes here and why? Which meant I did plenty of eavesdropping while waiting in lines, enjoying the sunshine on a mild yet brisk day. The first revealing conversation I overheard went something like this:

"When were we here last?" said a middle-aged, heavy-set woman wearing jeans, a fleecy pullover, and a backpack that likely had once belonged to one of her kids.

"Did we come last summer or the summer before?" asked a thin teenage girl, wearing tight jeans, a frilly blouse, and enough makeup for a modeling shoot.

"It was summer before last," said the third member of this party, presumably two parents and their daughter. "We came when Dolly was in the park, remember?"

"I wish we'd get to see her today," said the mother.

The daughter smirked and looked up from her phone. "Dolly's not gonna be here today! She's got better things to do. She's probably Christmas shopping in some big city or something. That's what I'd be doing if I had her money."

"Yeah, well, you don't," said the father. "And you don't

visiting her family in nearby Knoxville. These subsequent experiences confirmed the sense I'd gotten that first time: like its namesake, Dollywood was exceptional. It accurately reflects the dualities present in so much of Dolly herself.

On one hand it's a profitable, well-run business, providing thousands of jobs to this area where she grew up. The park is clean and bright, employees are friendly and helpful, and the amenities appeal to kids and adults alike. It's surprisingly educational and clearly intent on preserving the culture of mountain artisans, smiths, and crafters with authenticity and accuracy.

Dollywood is a showcase for the magic of Dolly's music, manners, and mountain mythology. Her rags-to-riches story figures prominently, but not in an intrusive or self-aggrandizing way. The diversity of her musical tastes and diverse songwriting and recording career resounds from the half-dozen performance venues in the park. The theme park's devotion to nostalgia and a romanticized vision of country livin' harkens back to simpler, albeit harder, times, a comforting escape in our often scary hyper-tech world.

I went back to Dollywood again while writing this book. I had never been there at Christmastime before and marveled like a little kid at the more than four thousand multicolored lights outlining virtually every surface in the park. There were so many Christmas lights—on trees, shrubbery, buildings, shops, rides, *everywhere*—I my expectations exceeded. Dollywood was nothing like what I remembered or what my wife—who had worked at Silver Dollar City one sweltering summer hawking funnel cakes and lemonade—remembered. Instead, it brought back my happy memories of the old Opryland in its heyday.

For one thing, it was much larger, brighter, and more dynamic. Beautiful landscaping, squeaky-clean sidewalks, new facilities, and kid-friendly amenities made me rejoice. Sure, it had plenty of country kitsch, cornpone humor, and hillbilly-themed merchandise. But it also offered an amazing bluegrass concert at an outdoor theater, historical information on Appalachia and the Smokies, and a natural preserve for bald eagles, which was just about the coolest thing I'd ever seen at a theme park.

It was only later, on the way home, with the girls sleeping across our laps and Daddy Jim and Libby talking softly in the front seat, that I realized how relieved I was. Dolly had not let me—and millions of other fans—down. She had not merely stuck her name on something for a buck. She had indeed created an experience, a most happy one at that. She had somehow managed to bring her Dolly magic to this place so close to where she was born and raised.

Eavesdropping at Dollywood

After that first visit to Dollywood with our kids, my wife and I returned a couple more times over the years, while

Baby Steps toward a Leap of Faith

I admit, I was skeptical. As we pulled into one of the massive, alphabetized parking lots that summer day, I began thinking about how curious it was that Dolly had always been a part of my life. She was a part of my childhood and figured into the story of how I proposed to my wife. And now here I was, with a wife, two little girls, a career, and a mortgage, shuffling in to Dolly's theme park along with thousands of other young families.

Part of my skepticism stemmed from my basis for comparison. I had grown up visiting Opryland USA in the late seventies and early eighties. Located in suburban Nashville, this amusement park was themed around all kinds of American music, but naturally leaned heavily on country and western. It had great rides, was large enough to get lost in for a day, and was close to where I lived, the perfect destination for school field trips and church youth groups. I had loved that place and was sad that it had declined in later years before closing in 1997.

Silver Dollar City, Dollywood's predecessor, had not impressed me and my college buddies the time or two we'd driven up from UT for the day, probably because we couldn't drink beer there. It seemed smaller, more contained, and definitely aimed at families, not rowdy college kids. When I'd heard that Dolly had partnered with its former owners, added to it, and unveiled it anew, I figured that nothing much had changed besides the name.

Boy, was I wrong! Maybe it was seeing it through my daughters' eyes or maybe it was just being glad at having

But Dolly loves surprising people. "I really wish you could have seen the looks on lawyer's and business manager's faces when I told them I wanted to start a theme park in the hills of my hometown in East Tennessee and call it Dollywood. They thought I had already taken the train to Crazywood!"[3]

Dolly knew it wasn't the most logical, strategic, profitable business decision. But she also had learned to trust her instincts. Ever since leaving the hollers of the Smoky Mountains, she had longed to give back to the land and people she loved there. As soon as she was able, she began conducting benefit concerts and establishing scholarship funds for students at her old high school. But she had a vision for something with a much larger, permanent impact, something that would provide jobs and bring in visitors, something that would combine her love of music with her gift for business.

Something like Dollywood.

Now I'm a Believer

Dotti and I took our two young daughters to Dollywood in the late nineties, and by then the park had been thriving for over a decade. We lived in Colorado at the time, but most of our extended family still lived in Tennessee. Dotti's father and stepmother, Daddy Jim and Libby as our girls called them, lived in Knoxville and couldn't wait to take our family to Dollywood.

of duplicating the success of their Silver Dollar City in Branson, Missouri. Using this same shiny name for their new acquisition, the Herschends invested over a million dollars in improvements and additions, including Craftsman's Valley, where artisans made and sold wares authentic to Appalachia, and the Silver Dollar Grist Mill, the first working mill of its kind built in Tennessee in over a hundred years.

Around the same time these improvements were being made to Silver Dollar City, Dolly began hinting at her dream for her own similar attraction back home in East Tennessee. She mentioned the idea to Barbara Walters in their 1982 interview. Apparently, while out in L.A. making movies, Dolly found her inspiration. In a *People* magazine interview, she later explained, "A few years back, when I first started seeing the Hollywood sign, I kept thinking how cute it would be if I could change the H to a D and see how long it would take anybody to notice. It just popped into my mind that it would be a good name for a park."[2]

It was a huge, unprecedented risk. With her keen intelligence and business savvy, Dolly was no doubt well aware of how other, somewhat comparable ventures had struggled or failed. And at this point in her career, it wasn't as if Dolly had played it safe—after all, she had risked a lot and scored big by leaving Porter for a solo career, branching out beyond country music, and getting into the movies and TV. But still, a *theme park*?

Before Dollywood

Looking back, the creation of Dollywood seems inevitable. In 1961, brothers Harry and Grover Robbins, two area entrepreneurs from North Carolina, opened an attraction designed to capitalize on the centennial of the Civil War and Southern sympathies for the Confederacy. The attraction's centerpiece was an operational coal-fired steam train that took visitors on a five-mile loop at the edge of the Smokies, complete with theatrical attacks from Yankees and Indians. By our standards today, it was probably the most unpolitically correct theme park imaginable.[1]

In 1970, the attraction was purchased by Art Modell, a millionaire businessman and owner of the NFL's Cleveland Browns. Shifting the Confederate theme to a broader mountain-pioneering motif, the park became Goldrush Junction, keeping Klondike Katie, as the train became known, and expanding the village complete with general store, saloon, blacksmith shop, and costumed employees. A woodshop, sawmill, and outdoor theater were also added. The most significant addition, however, foreshadowed the park's famous future owner. In 1973, the Robert F. Thomas Church opened its doors as a tribute to the renowned local doctor who had delivered Sevier County's most famous resident in exchange for a bag of cornmeal.

A few years later, the park changed owners and its name once again. Another pair of enterprising brothers, Jack and Pete Herschend, bought the property in hopes and iconic movies forming the pillars of its parks. It continues to unveil new additions based on its latest hit, most recently *Frozen*, as well as acquire existing franchises, such as *Star Wars*.

And then there's Dollywood.

While it's often called the redneck Disneyland, most fans agree—surely the ones who have been there—that there is nothing else quite like Dollywood. It's about more than just the life and career of Dolly Parton, although as a singer, songwriter, entertainer, movie star, producer, and entrepreneur, her life does provide a wealth of material. Simply put, it's about the experience of being there. As the park's trademarked motto explains, "We create memories worth repeating."

A big part of it has to do with the setting—the Great Smoky Mountains of East Tennessee. The location has become synonymous with Southern Appalachia and the pioneering lifestyle of the mountain folk who settled there. Their culture provides a rich tapestry with many colorful strands of history, art, music, and storytelling. And, of course, there's the breathtaking beauty of the Smokies, so named because of the way misty vapors of fog rise like smoke from the densely wooded vistas. With over nine million visitors annually, the Great Smoky Mountains National Park, created in 1934 under President Franklin D. Roosevelt, is the most visited national park in the US—which doesn't hurt when you're hoping to attract visitors to a new theme park.

The Faith of Dolly Parton

Dolly surely knows this, considering the numerous risks she has taken throughout her career. Still, I can only imagine what it must have been like when she told her accountants, advisors, and team members of a certain risk she wanted to take—her biggest one yet. "You want to do *what?*" I can hear them saying.

And I have to say, it really was a crazy idea.

For perspective, just imagine your favorite celebrity, performer, or entertainer other than Dolly. Now imagine a place devoted to this person; acres and acres focused on all that he or she's accomplished, as well as all they care about and believe in. Can you see it? What does it look like? And what would it be called? GarthWorld? Carrie's UnderWoods? Adeleville? It's silly to even consider, right?

Conway's Twitty City; Barbara Mandrell's home, Fontanel Mansion; and Loretta Lynn's Hurricane Mills, all in the Nashville area, can't really compare. While there's Graceland, Elvis's home-turned-shrine in Memphis, and Jimmy Buffett's Margaritaville hotel and restaurant, as well as numerous small landmarks and makeshift museums honoring everyone from John Philip Sousa to Led Zeppelin, it's hard to imagine any other celebrity sustaining an entire theme park around their image, brand, values, and body of work.

Disney World and Disneyland certainly seem to set the standard for thematic brand parks, but they don't revolve around one person, one story, or one cast of characters. Disney has a vault of iconic cartoons, beloved characters,

CHAPTER 6

Baby Steps toward a Leap of Faith

I have taken some mighty big chances in my life. Some of them have worked out, some haven't. However, every time I have stepped out of my comfort zone, I have learned a ton of valuable lessons—lessons that helped me in all parts of my life.
DOLLY PARTON

Go big or go home.
We've all heard this or some variation of this down-home declaration. But what I'm learning is that it has a basis in the Bible! Scripture shows repeatedly that God requires us to step out in faith and take some big risks. Faith in itself is often a challenge to what appears logical, probable, or possible. But that's when we have to remember that God has a much bigger perspective—the most comprehensive of all.

Practice More Than You Preach

🦋 How does Dolly describe this "Old Time Preacher Man," based on her own grandfather, Reverend Jake Owens? What impact do you think growing up in the church (and having a preacher for her grandpa!) had on Dolly? On her attitudes toward giving and forgiving?

🦋 What experiences with organized religion, the church, or a minister from your own life came to mind as you listened to this song? What impact have they had on your faith today?

Dear God,

You are so gracious and generous to me—thank you! I'm so grateful for the many blessings in my life and acknowledge you as the source of all I have. I am your steward and want to share with others so that they might know you and your love. Help me to be like Dolly, who gives so generously and always with a cheerful heart. Give me strength to forgive the people who hurt me or seek to cause harm against me. Remind me that just as you forgive me, I can forgive them.

Amen.

Divine Dose of Dolly

Dear children, let us not love with words or speech but with actions and in truth.
       1 JOHN 3:18

🦋 Do you generally think of yourself as a generous person? Why or why not? How often do you put conditions on your willingness to give or, like me sometimes, justify not giving at all? Is this the kind of person you want to be? Better still, is this the kind of person God wants you to be?

🦋 What inspires you most about Dolly's generosity and willingness to forgive others? Why? How can you follow her example in your life today? Who do you need to forgive in order to obey God and to move on in your life? Don't put it off—call them, visit them, write them right now!

Listen to Dolly sing "Daddy Was an Old Time Preacher Man," a song she says was inspired by her "fire and brimstone" preaching Pentecostal maternal grandfather. Then answer the following questions.

Practice More Than You Preach

Dolly seems to have taken this to heart, which is only fitting. She was always one of my daddy's favorite singers, especially while she was on *The Porter Wagoner Show*. I remember him humming along to one of their duets, a song called, as I later learned, "The Pain of Loving You."

Dolly and Katy Perry attend the 51st Academy of Country Music Awards, 2016.

Dolly sings "Jolene" in Pittsburgh, 2016.

Dolly headlined the 1987–1988 prime-time variety show, *Dolly!*

Performing at the 43rd Annual Grammy Awards, 2001

Dolly, 1984

Dolly at Dollywood, 1988

Dolly in one of her most famous movie roles, 1982.

Performing on stage at The Dominion Theatre, London, 1983.

Belting out a tune, 1977.

Dolly behind the wheel, 1982

Dolly showing her goofy side, 1976.

Les Paul, Dolly Parton, Chet Atkins, and Freddie Fisher at the Grammy Awards in the Hollywood Palladium, 1977.

Dolly, circa 1966

Dolly croons at a performance, 1970.

Dolly, age 3

Dolly Parton at age fourteen from Sevier County High School, 1960